SpongeBob SquarePants™

GONE JELLYFISHIN'

Senior Editor - Elizabeth Hurchalla
Contributing Editors - Bailey Murphy and Amy Court Kaemon
Graphic Designer and Letterer - Tomás Montalvo-Lagos
Cover Designer - Raymond Makowski
Graphic Artist - Tomás Montalvo-Lagos

Digital Imaging Manager - Chris Buford
Pre-Press Manager - Antonio DePietro
Production Managers - Jennifer Miller and Mutsumi Miyazaki
Senior Designer - Anna Kernbaum
Art Director - Matt Alford
Managing Editor - Jill Freshney
VP of Production - Ron Klamert
Editor in Chief - Mike Kiley
President & C.O.O. - John Parker
Publisher & C.E.O. - Stuart Levy

E-mail: info@TOKYOPOP.com
Come visit us online at www.TOKYOPOP.com

A ⊙ TOKYOPOP® Cine-Manga®
TOKYOPOP Inc.
5900 Wilshire Blvd., Suite 2000
Los Angeles, CA 90036

SpongeBob SquarePants: Gone Jellyfishing

ISBN: 1-59532-678-2

First TOKYOPOP® printing: February 2005

10 9 8 7 6 5 4 3 2 1

Printed in the USA

NICKELODEON

SpongeBob SquarePants™

Created by Stephen Hillenburg

GONE JELLYFISHIN'

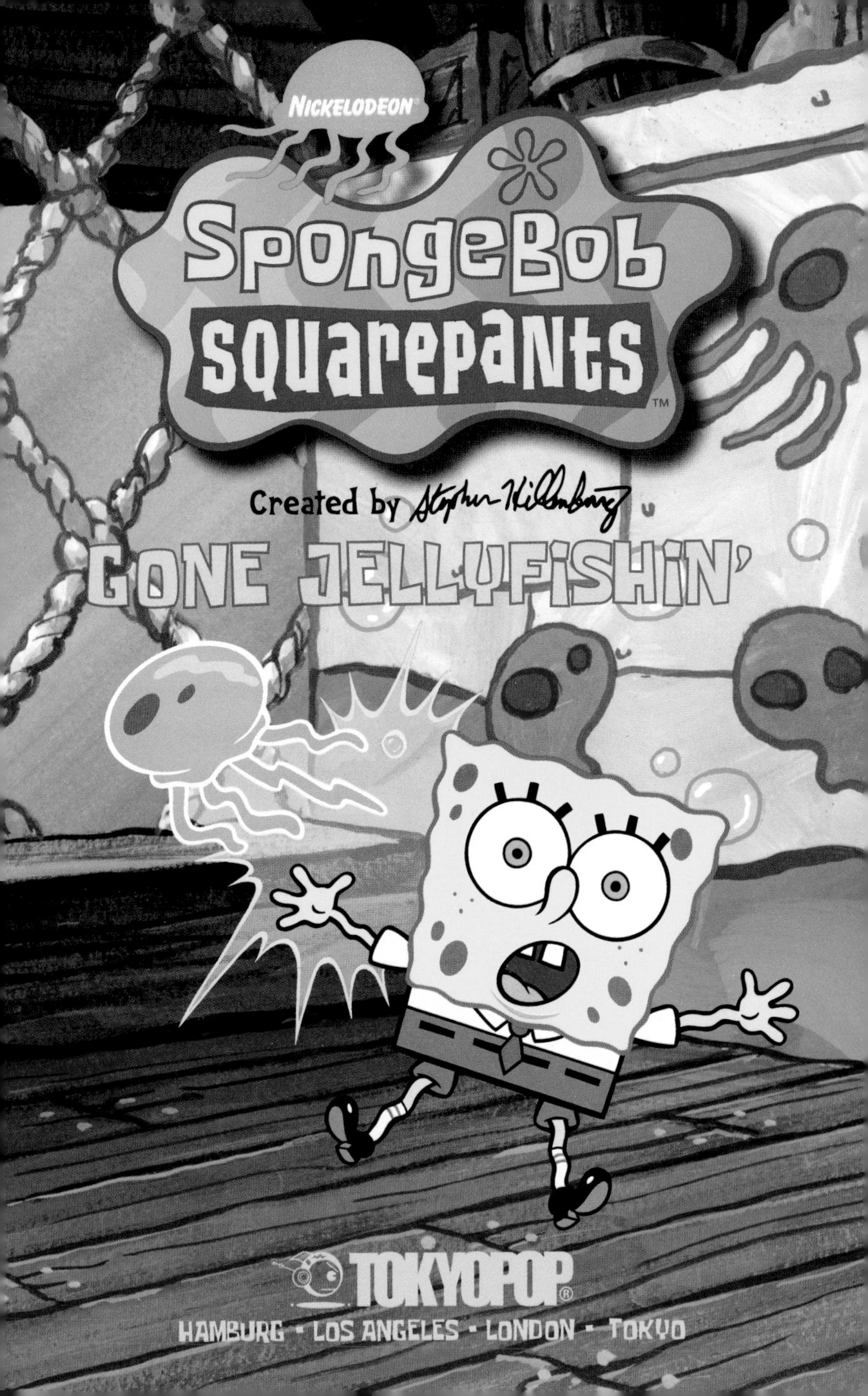

TOKYOPOP®

HAMBURG • LOS ANGELES • LONDON • TOKYO

NICKELODEON

SpongeBob
SQUAREPANTS ™

SPONGEBOB SQUAREPANTS: An optimistic and friendly sea sponge who lives in a pineapple with his snail, Gary, and works as a fry cook at The Krusty Krab. He loves his job and is always looking on the bright side of everything.

PATRICK STAR: A starfish who is SpongeBob's best friend and neighbor.

GARY: SpongeBob's pet snail. Meows like a cat.

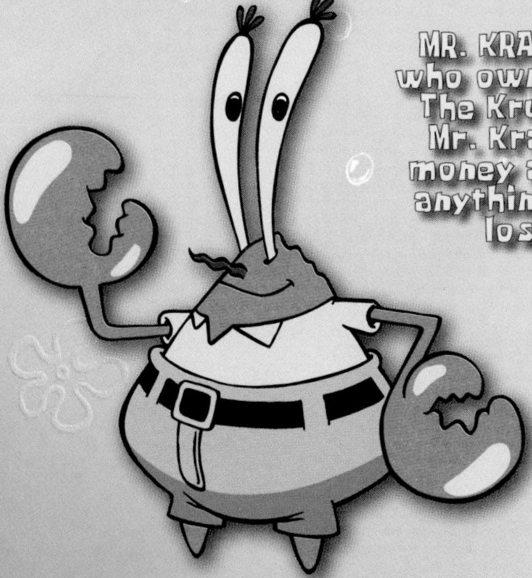

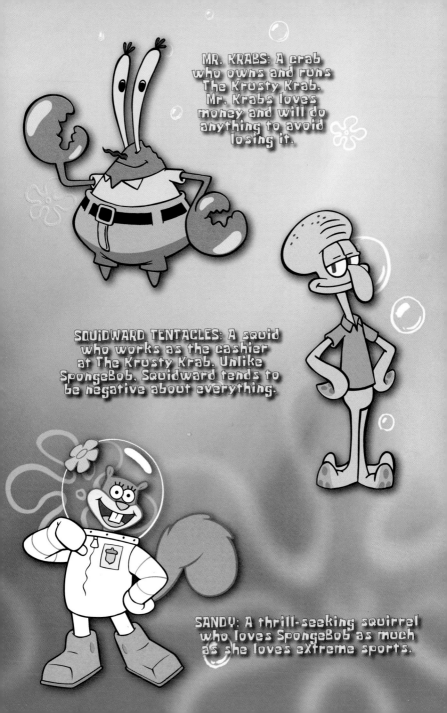

MR. KRABS: A crab who owns and runs The Krusty Krab. Mr. Krabs loves money and will do anything to avoid losing it.

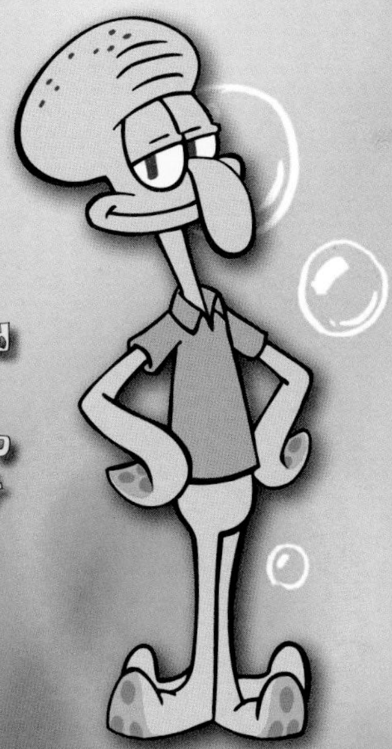

SQUIDWARD TENTACLES: A squid who works as the cashier at The Krusty Krab. Unlike SpongeBob, Squidward tends to be negative about everything.

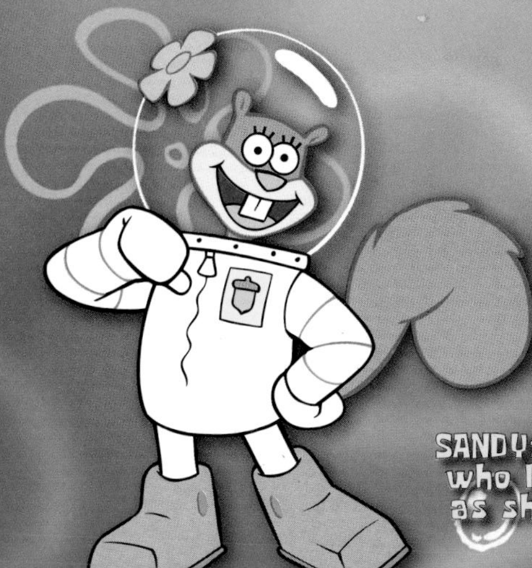

SANDY: A thrill-seeking squirrel who loves SpongeBob as much as she loves eXtreme sports.

SpongeBob SquarePants

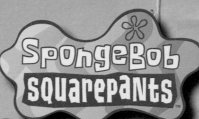

GONE JELLYFISHIN'

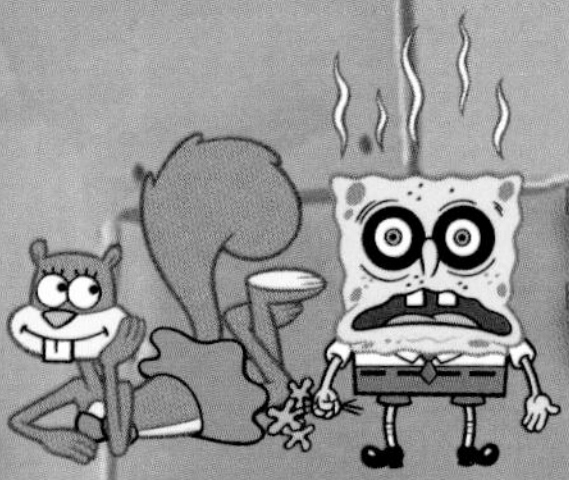

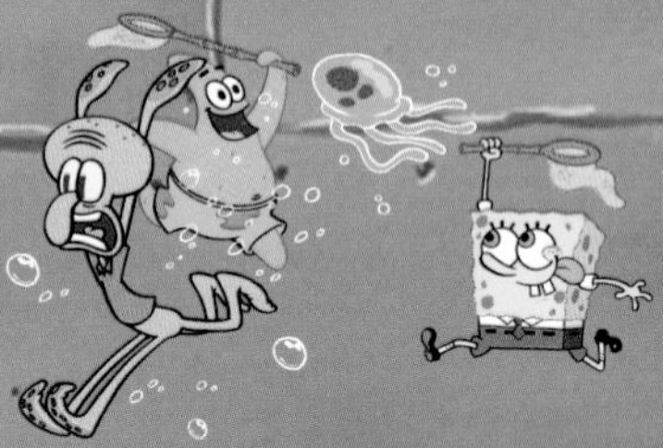

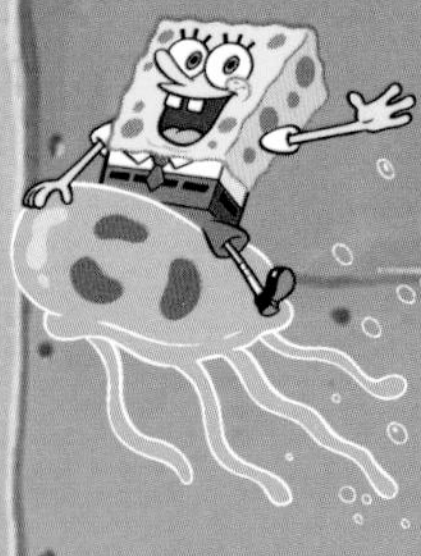

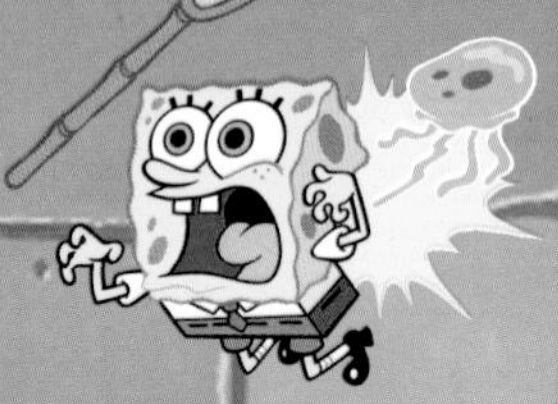

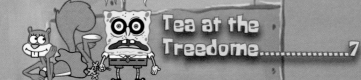

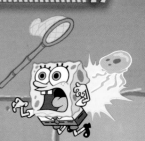

SpongeBob SquarePants

Tea at the Treedome

by Peter Burns, Mr. Lawrence
and Paul Tibbitt

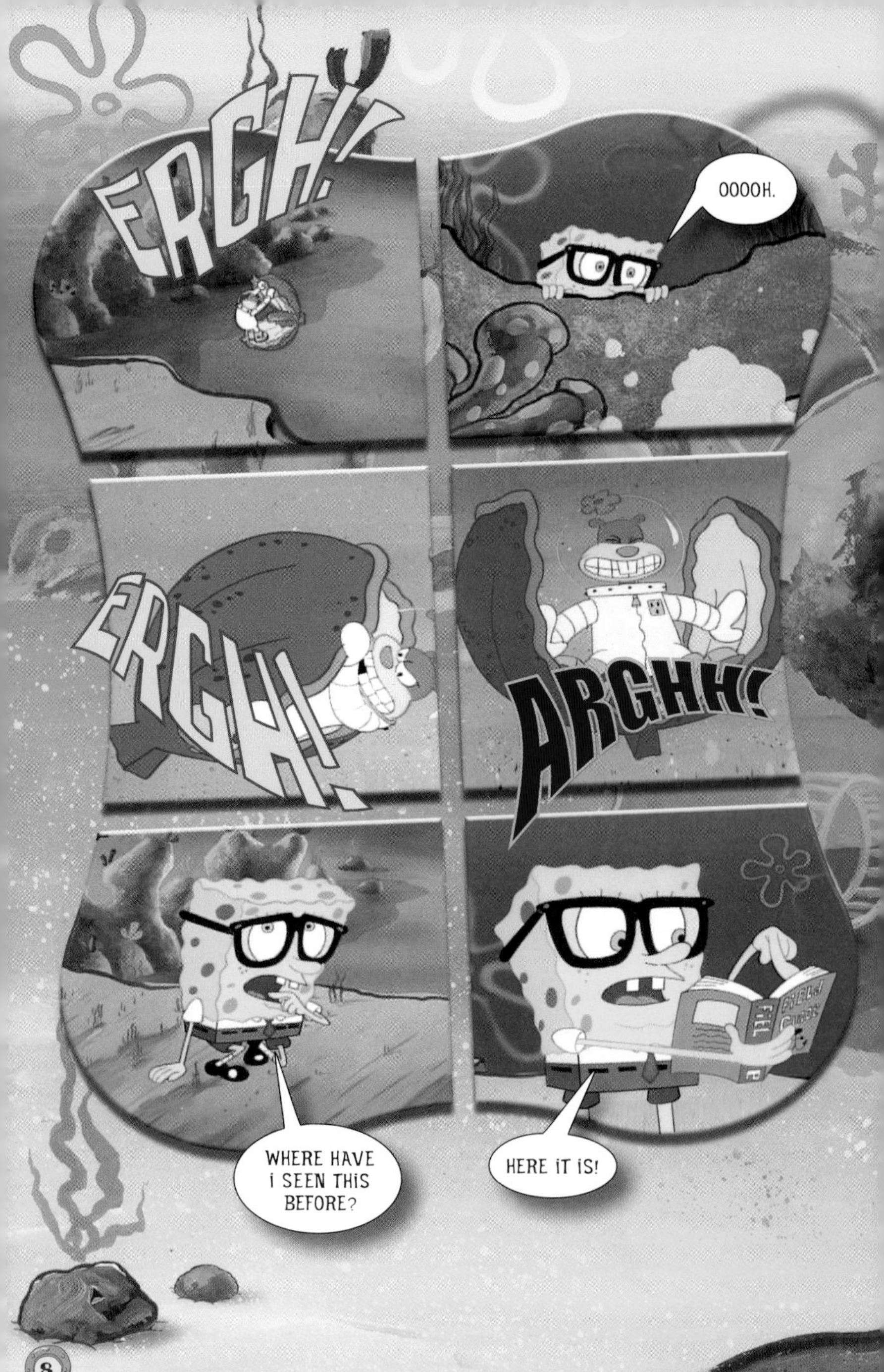
ERGH!
OOOOH.
ERGH!
ARGHH!
WHERE HAVE I SEEN THIS BEFORE?
HERE IT IS!

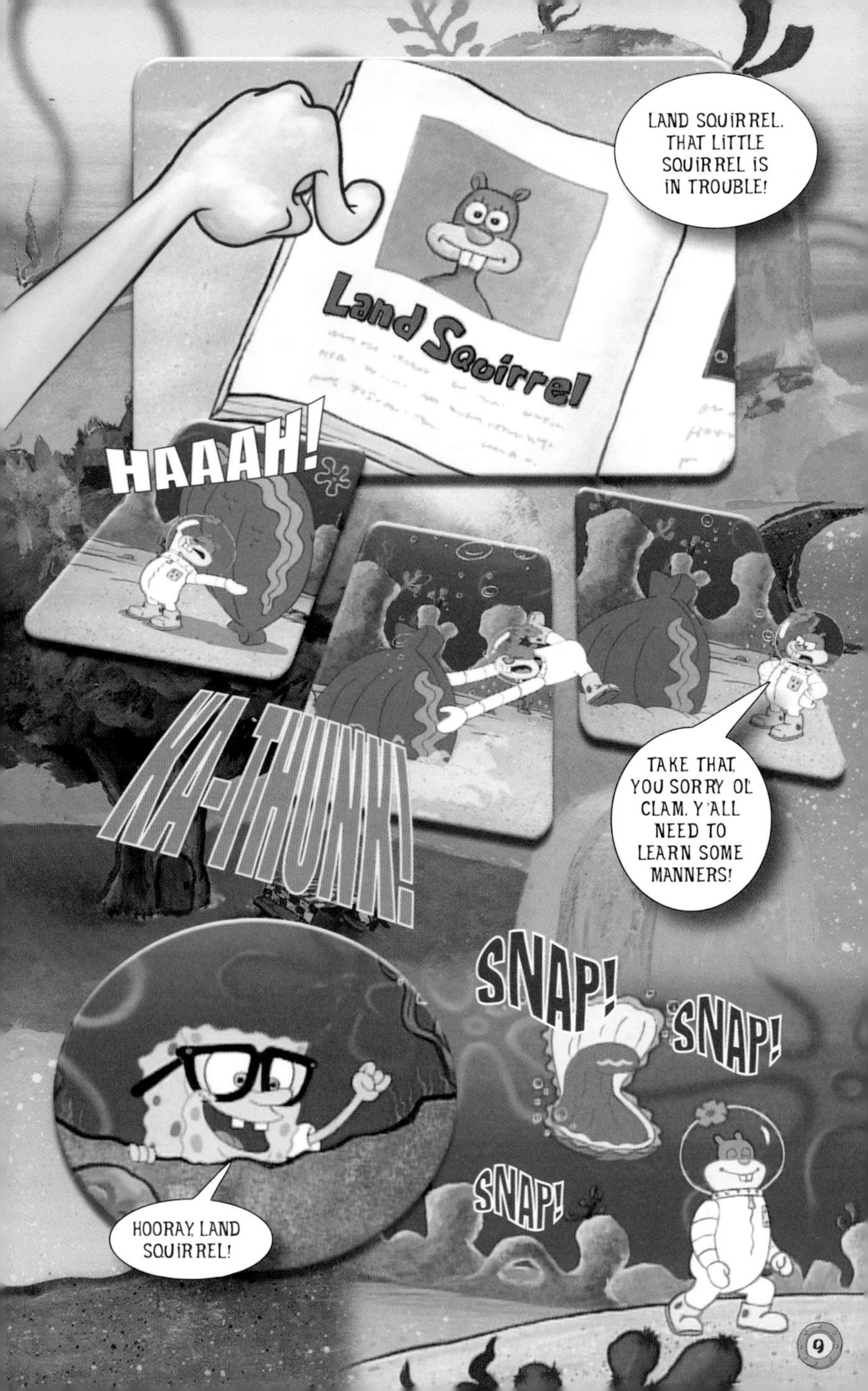
Land Squirrel
LAND SQUIRREL. THAT LITTLE SQUIRREL IS IN TROUBLE!
HAAAH!
KA-THUNK!
TAKE THAT, YOU SORRY OL' CLAM. Y'ALL NEED TO LEARN SOME MANNERS!
SNAP!
SNAP!
SNAP!
HOORAY, LAND SQUIRREL!

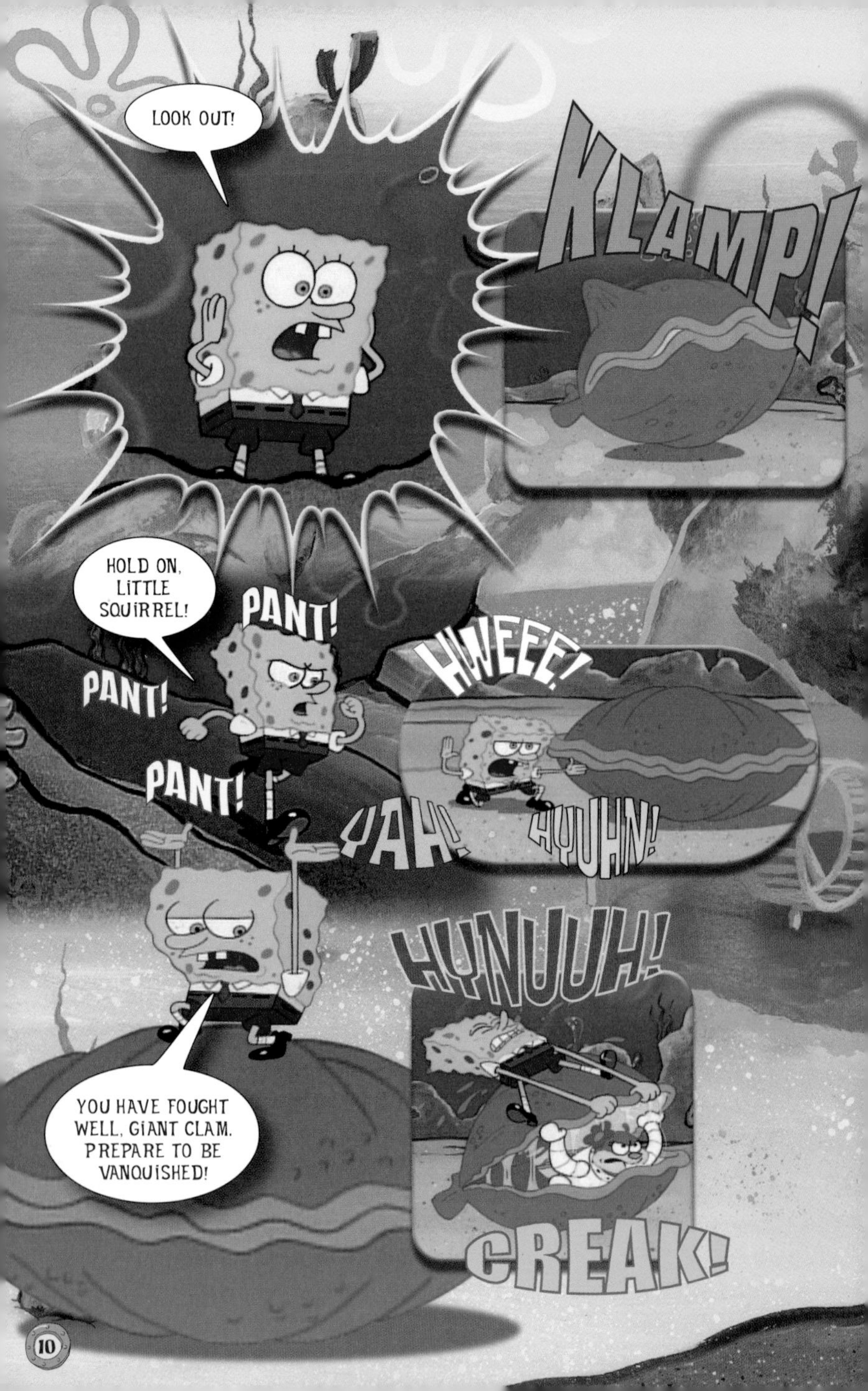

LOOK OUT!
KLAMP!
HOLD ON, LITTLE SQUIRREL!
PANT!
PANT!
PANT!
HWEEE!
YAH!
HYUHN!
YOU HAVE FOUGHT WELL, GIANT CLAM. PREPARE TO BE VANQUISHED!
HYNUUH!
CREAK!

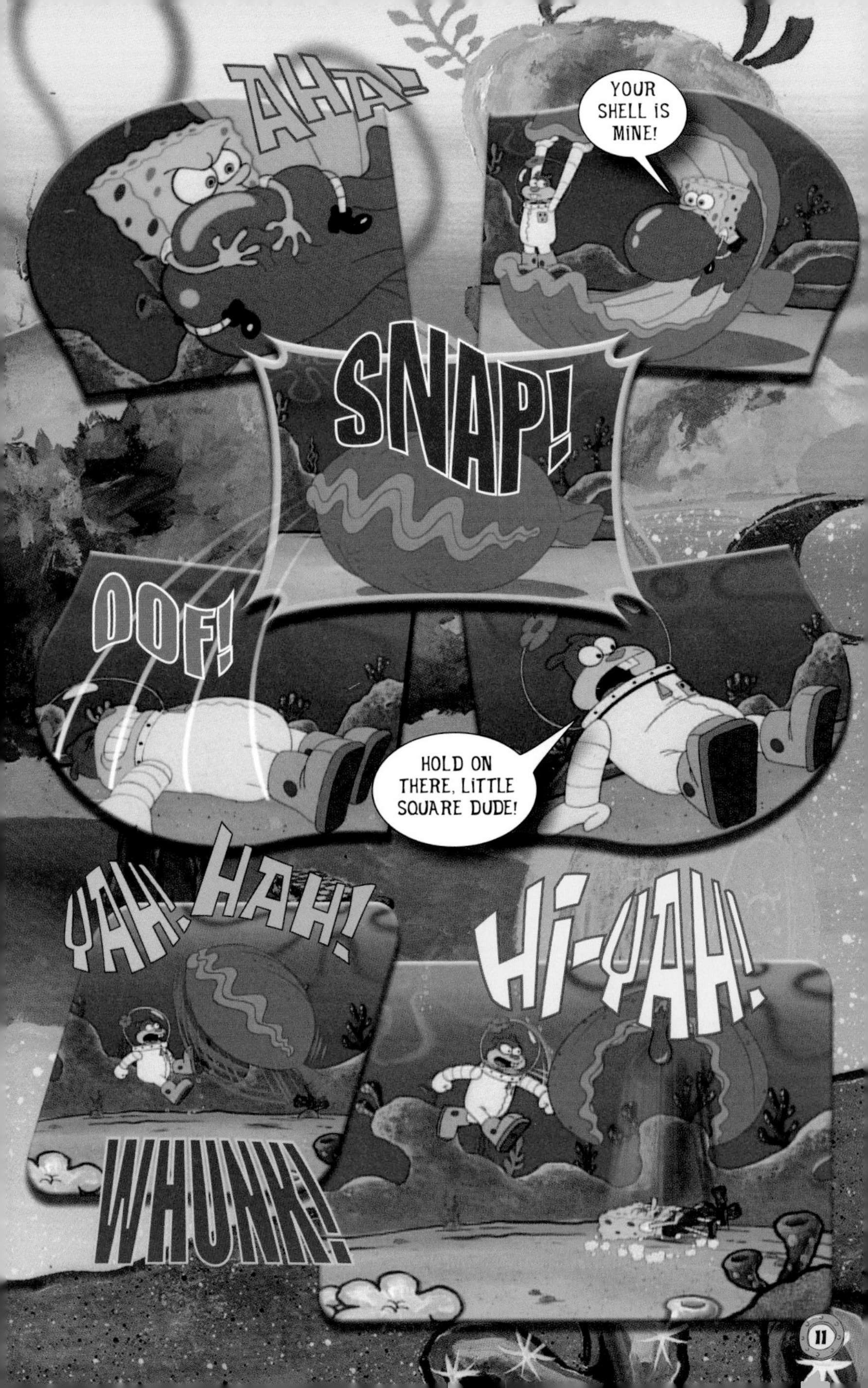

AHA!
YOUR SHELL IS MINE!
SNAP!
OOF!
HOLD ON THERE, LITTLE SQUARE DUDE!
YAH! HAH!
HI-YAH!
WHUNK!

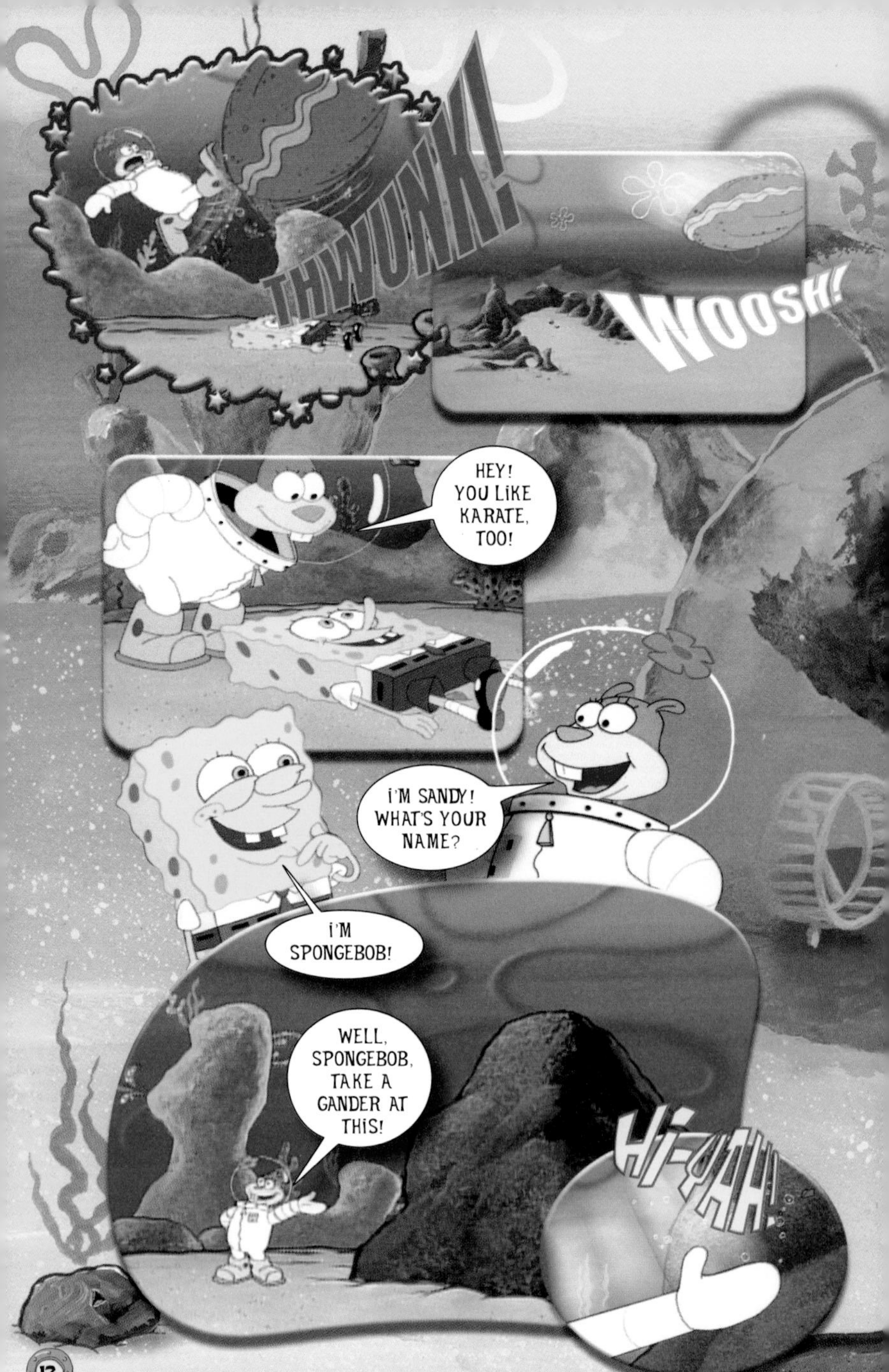
THWUNK!
WOOSH!
HEY! YOU LIKE KARATE, TOO!
I'M SANDY! WHAT'S YOUR NAME?
I'M SPONGEBOB!
WELL, SPONGEBOB, TAKE A GANDER AT THIS!
HI-YAH!

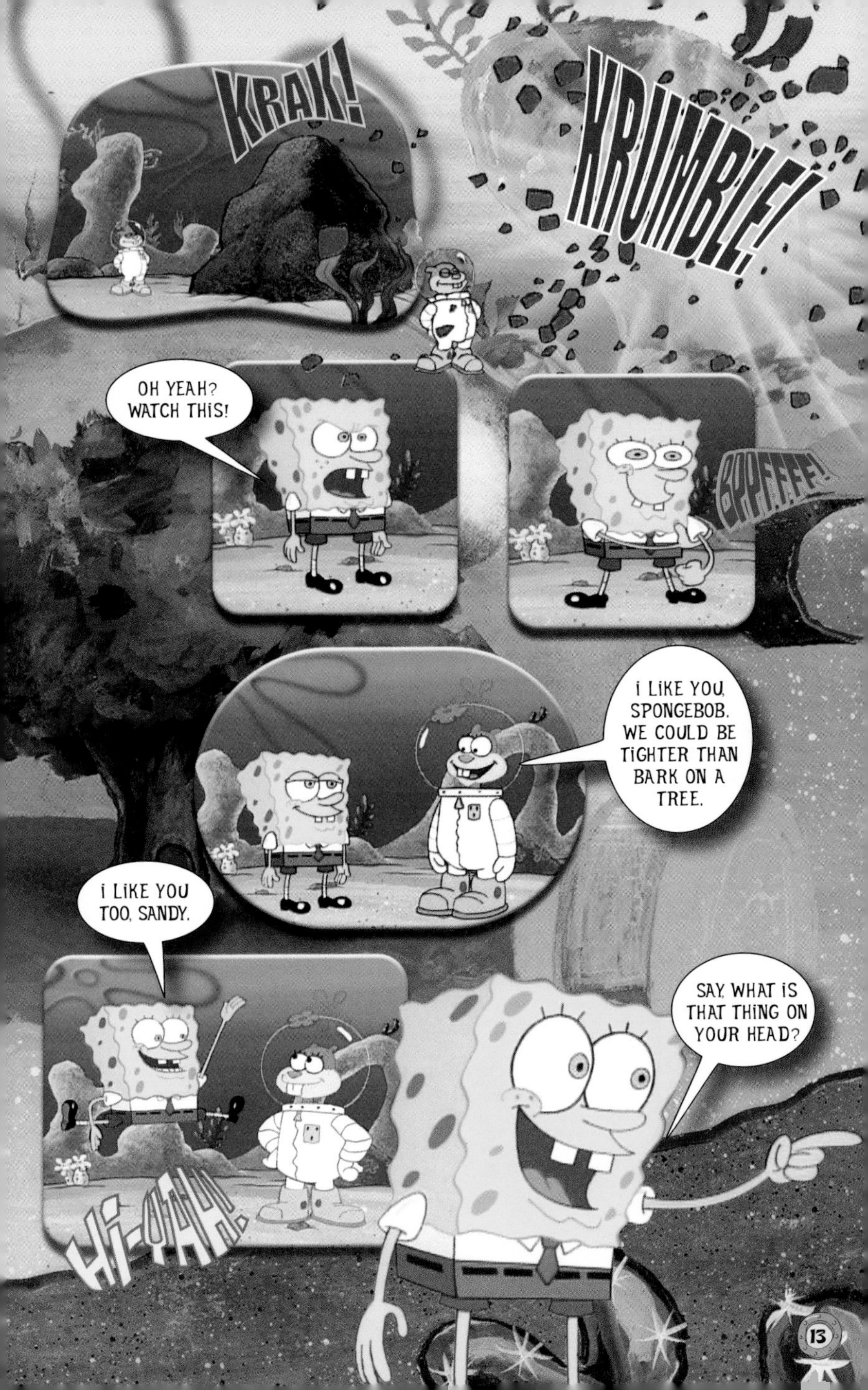
KRAK!
KRUMBLE!
OH YEAH? WATCH THIS!
BOFFFF!
I LIKE YOU, SPONGEBOB. WE COULD BE TIGHTER THAN BARK ON A TREE.
I LIKE YOU TOO, SANDY.
SAY, WHAT IS THAT THING ON YOUR HEAD?

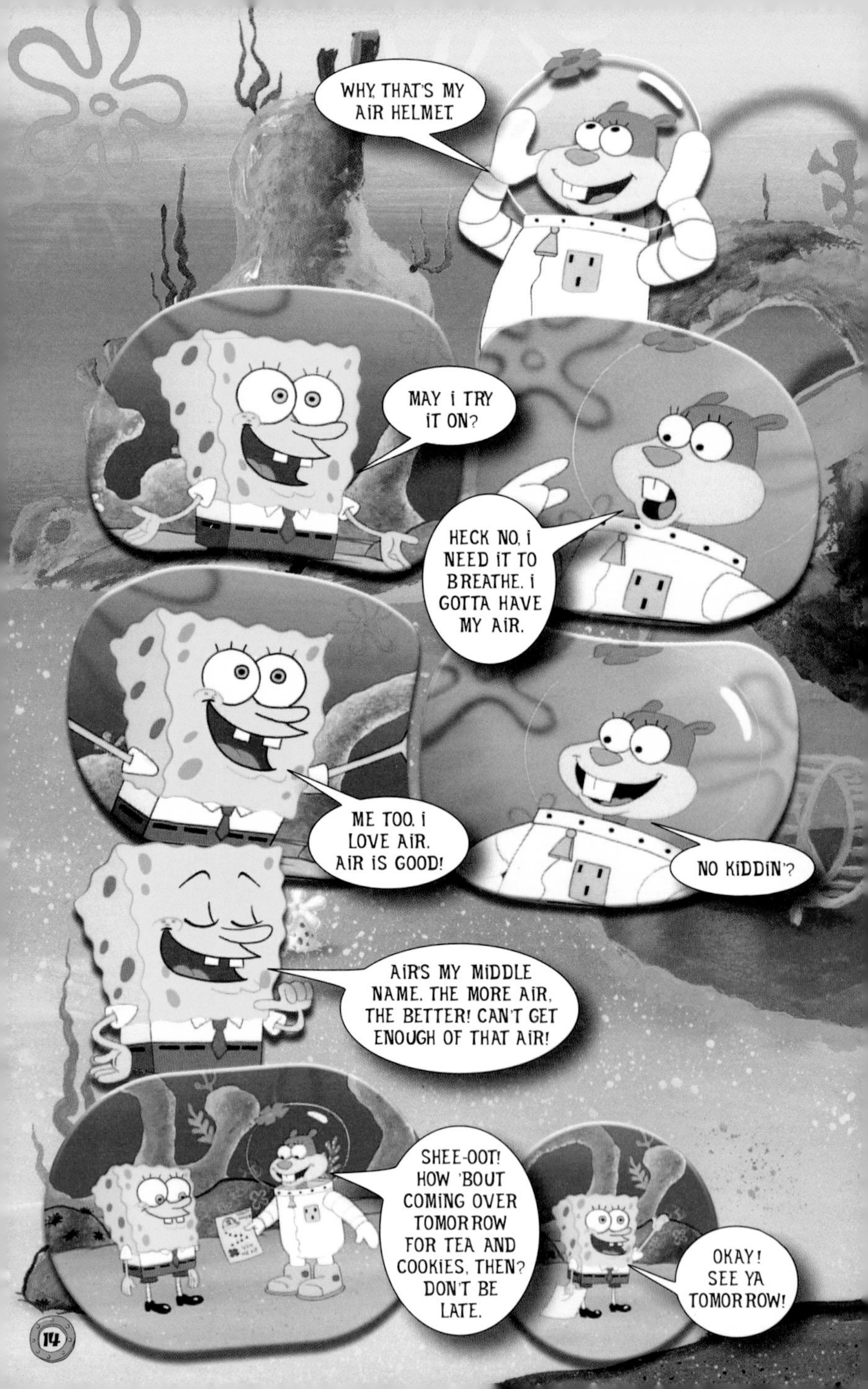

WHY, THAT'S MY AIR HELMET.
MAY I TRY IT ON?
HECK NO, I NEED IT TO BREATHE. I GOTTA HAVE MY AIR.
ME TOO. I LOVE AIR. AIR IS GOOD!
NO KIDDIN'?
AIR'S MY MIDDLE NAME. THE MORE AIR, THE BETTER! CAN'T GET ENOUGH OF THAT AIR!
SHEE-OOT! HOW 'BOUT COMING OVER TOMORROW FOR TEA AND COOKIES, THEN? DON'T BE LATE.
OKAY! SEE YA TOMORROW!

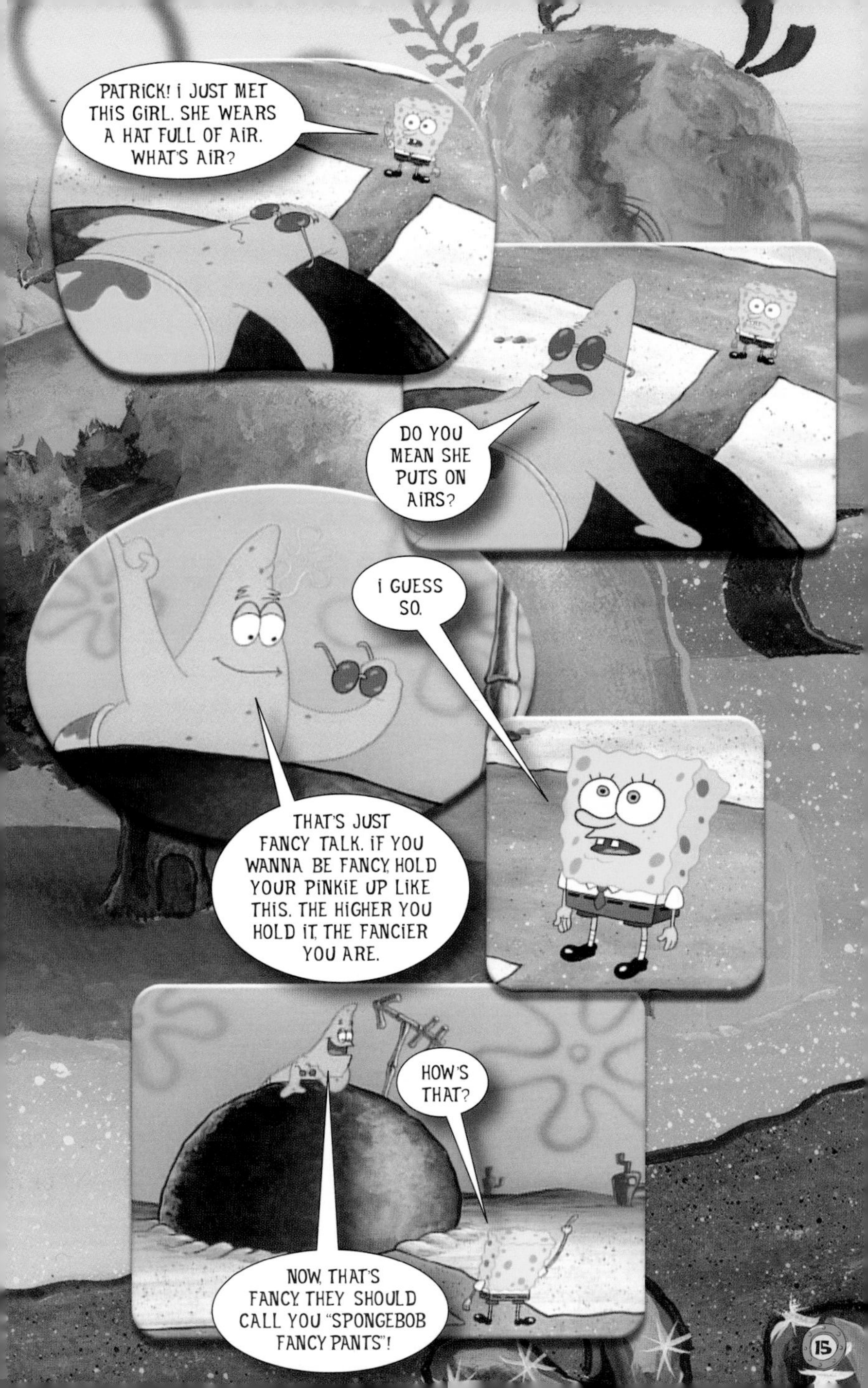
PATRICK! i JUST MET THIS GIRL. SHE WEARS A HAT FULL OF AiR. WHAT'S AiR?
DO YOU MEAN SHE PUTS ON AiRS?
i GUESS SO.
THAT'S JUST FANCY TALK. iF YOU WANNA BE FANCY, HOLD YOUR PiNKiE UP LiKE THIS. THE HiGHER YOU HOLD iT, THE FANCiER YOU ARE.
HOW'S THAT?
NOW, THAT'S FANCY. THEY SHOULD CALL YOU "SPONGEBOB FANCY PANTS"!

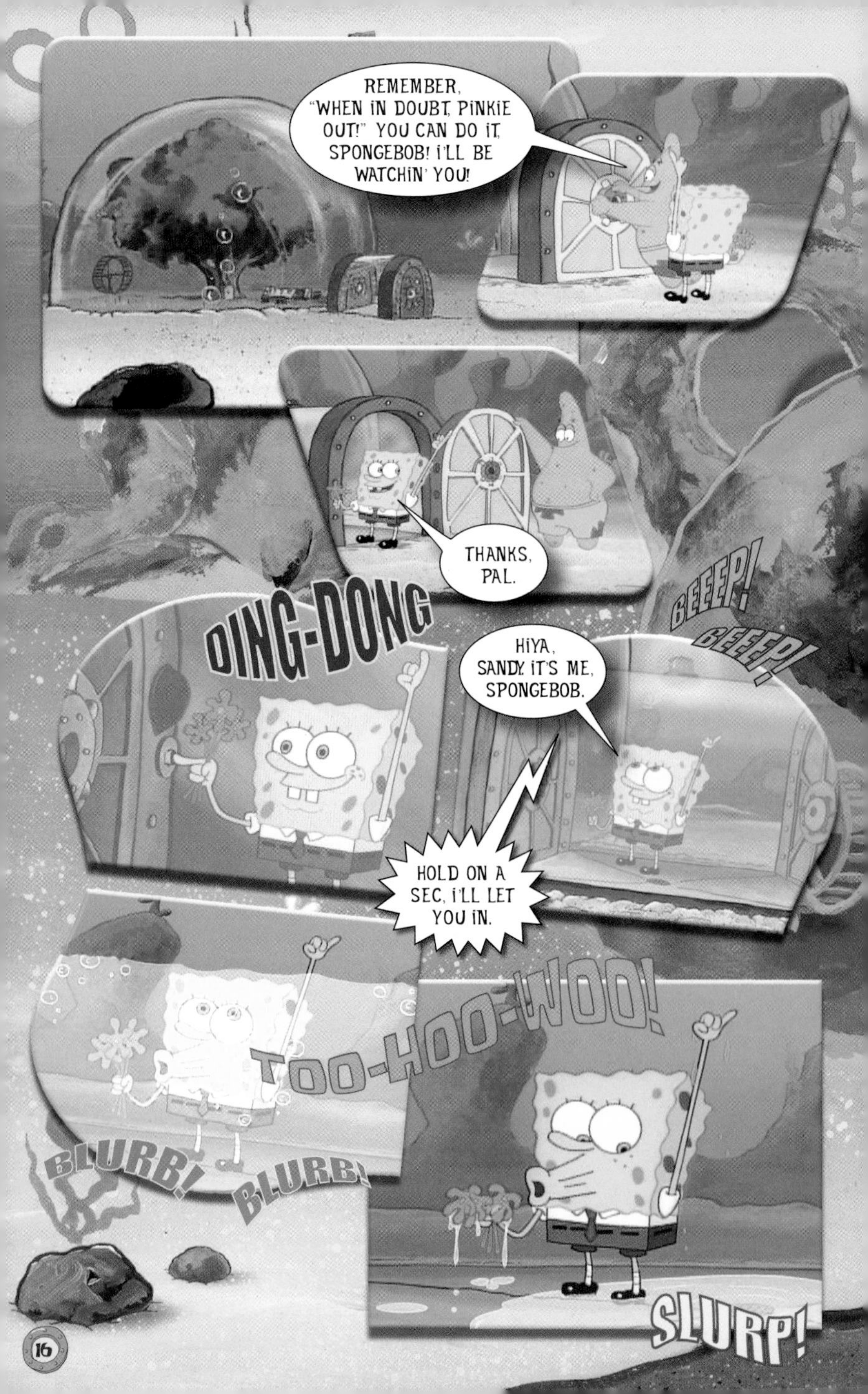
REMEMBER, "WHEN IN DOUBT, PINKIE OUT!" YOU CAN DO IT, SPONGEBOB! I'LL BE WATCHIN' YOU!
THANKS, PAL.
DING-DONG
BEEEP! BEEEP!
HIYA, SANDY. IT'S ME, SPONGEBOB.
HOLD ON A SEC, I'LL LET YOU IN.
TOO-HOO-WOO!
BLURB! BLURB!
SLURP!

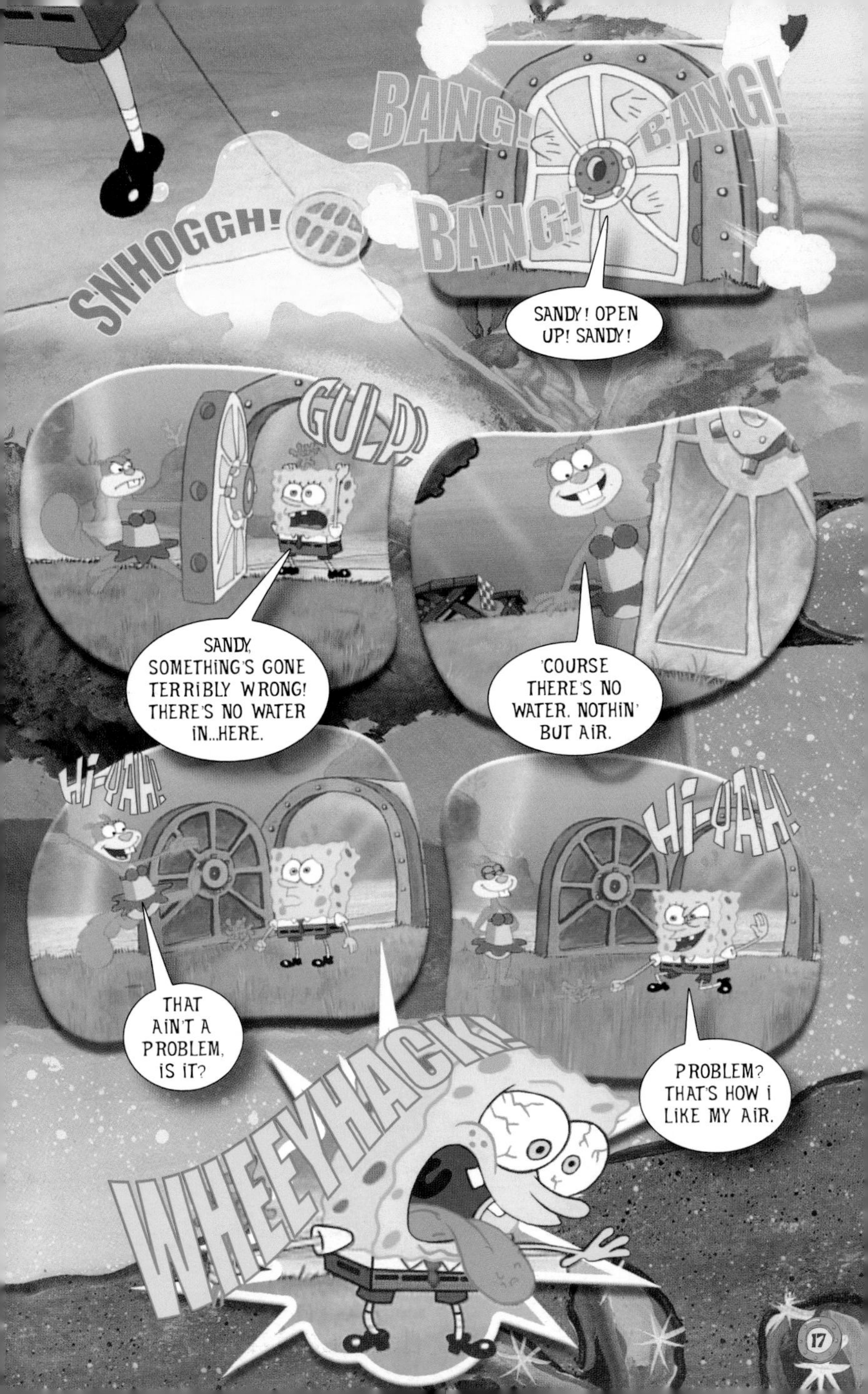
SNHOGGH!
BANG!
BANG!
BANG!
SANDY! OPEN UP! SANDY!
GULP!
SANDY, SOMETHING'S GONE TERRIBLY WRONG! THERE'S NO WATER IN...HERE.
'COURSE THERE'S NO WATER. NOTHIN' BUT AIR.
HI-YAH!
THAT AIN'T A PROBLEM, IS IT?
HI-YAH!
PROBLEM? THAT'S HOW I LIKE MY AIR.
WHEEYHACK!

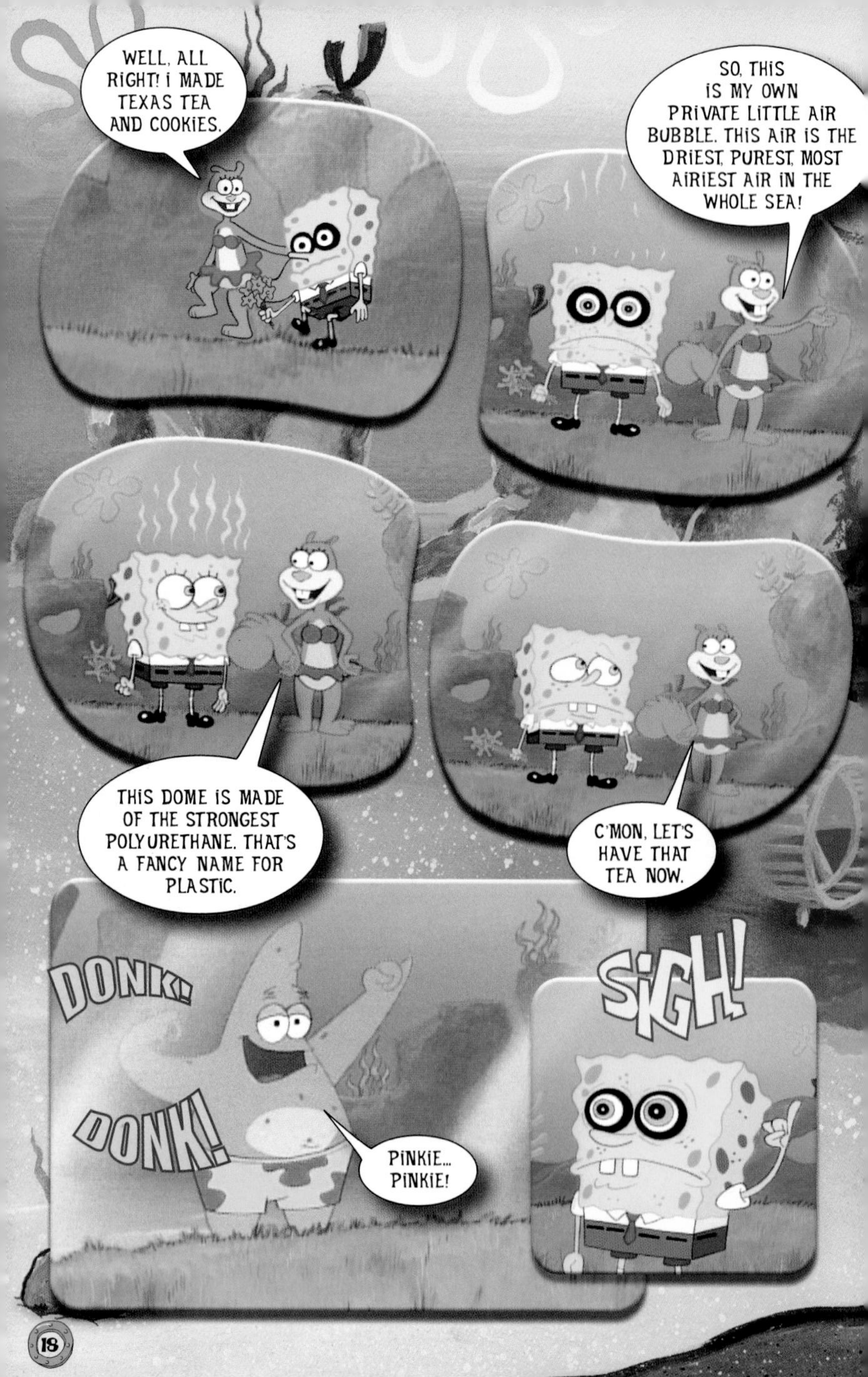
WELL, ALL RIGHT! I MADE TEXAS TEA AND COOKIES.
SO, THIS IS MY OWN PRIVATE LITTLE AIR BUBBLE. THIS AIR IS THE DRIEST, PUREST, MOST AIRIEST AIR IN THE WHOLE SEA!
THIS DOME IS MADE OF THE STRONGEST POLYURETHANE. THAT'S A FANCY NAME FOR PLASTIC.
C'MON, LET'S HAVE THAT TEA NOW.
DONK!
DONK!
PINKIE... PINKIE!
SIGH!

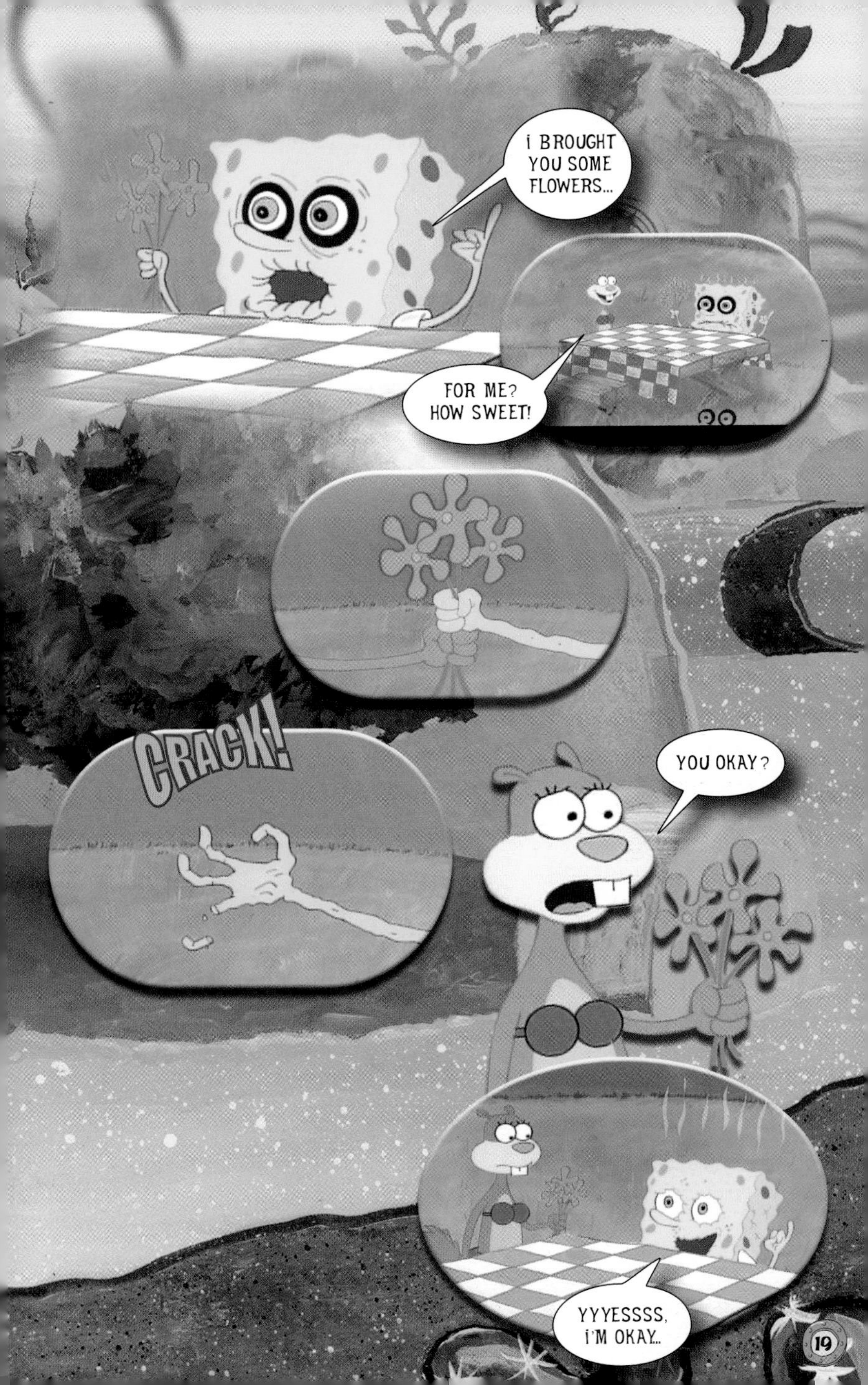
I BROUGHT YOU SOME FLOWERS...
FOR ME? HOW SWEET!
CRACK!
YOU OKAY?
YYYESSSS, I'M OKAY...

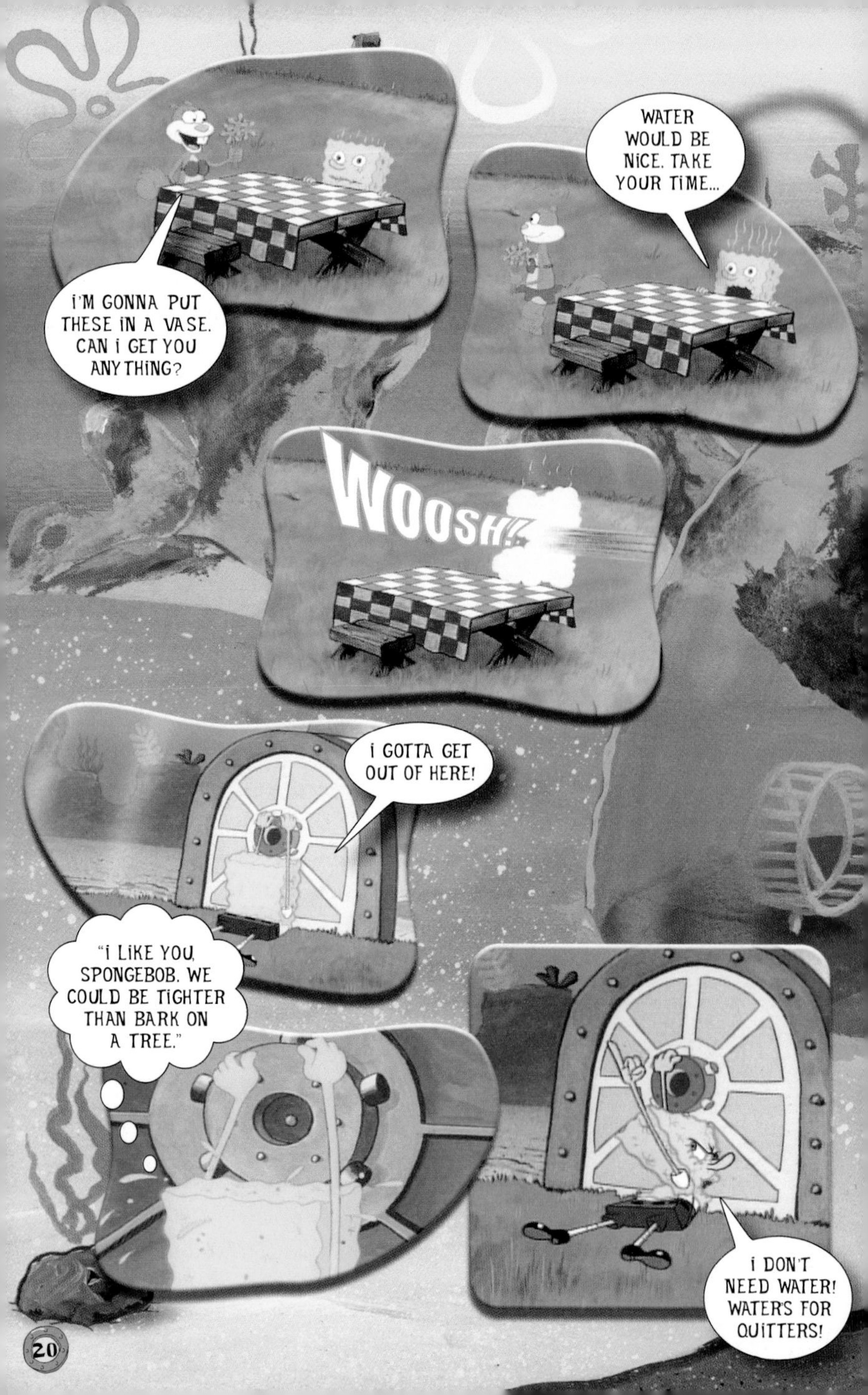
I'M GONNA PUT THESE IN A VASE. CAN I GET YOU ANYTHING?
WATER WOULD BE NICE. TAKE YOUR TIME...
WOOSH!
I GOTTA GET OUT OF HERE!
"I LIKE YOU, SPONGEBOB. WE COULD BE TIGHTER THAN BARK ON A TREE."
I DON'T NEED WATER! WATER'S FOR QUITTERS!

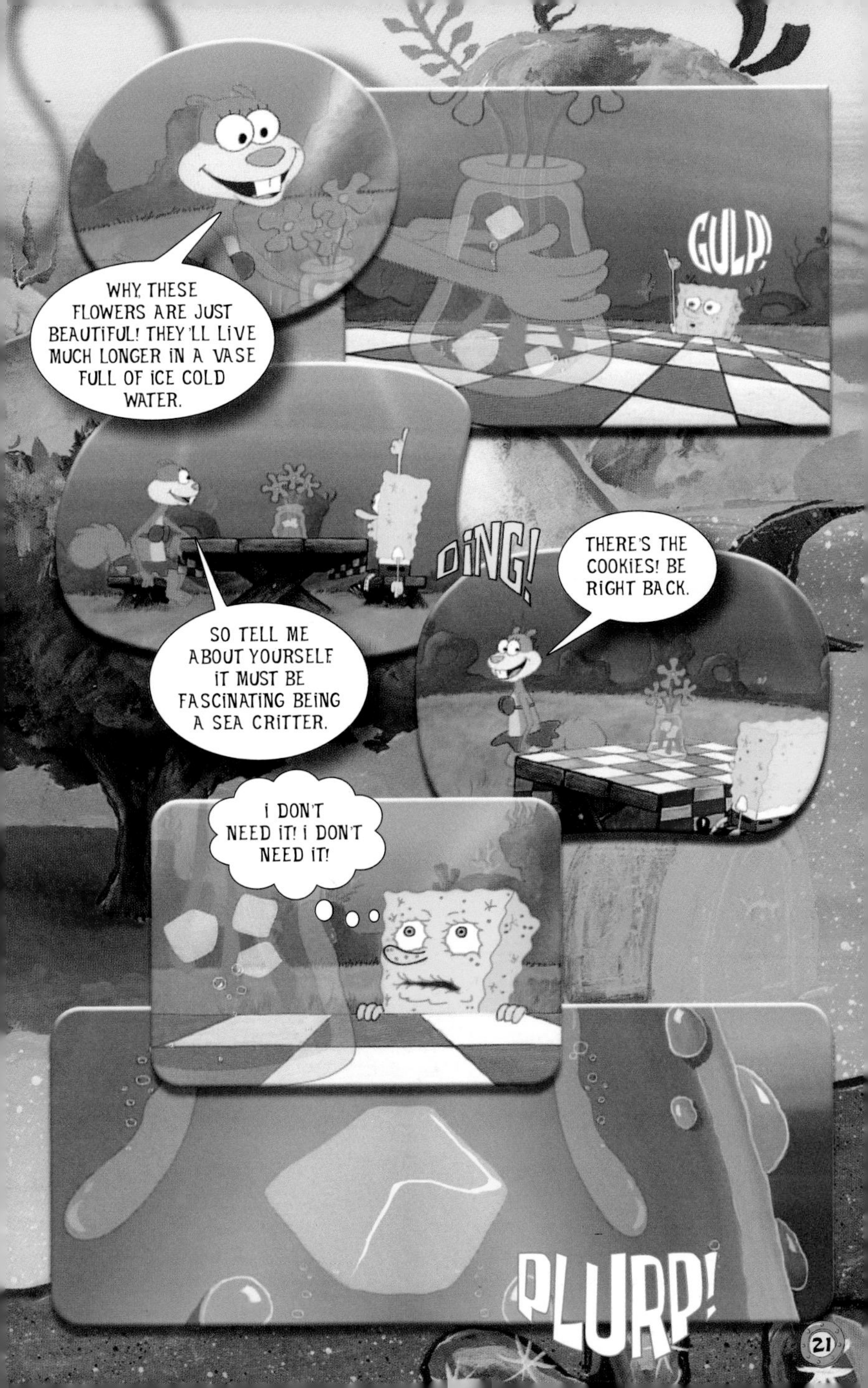
WHY, THESE FLOWERS ARE JUST BEAUTIFUL! THEY'LL LIVE MUCH LONGER IN A VASE FULL OF ICE COLD WATER.
GULP!
SO TELL ME ABOUT YOURSELF. IT MUST BE FASCINATING BEING A SEA CRITTER.
DING!
THERE'S THE COOKIES! BE RIGHT BACK.
I DON'T NEED IT! I DON'T NEED IT!
PLURP!

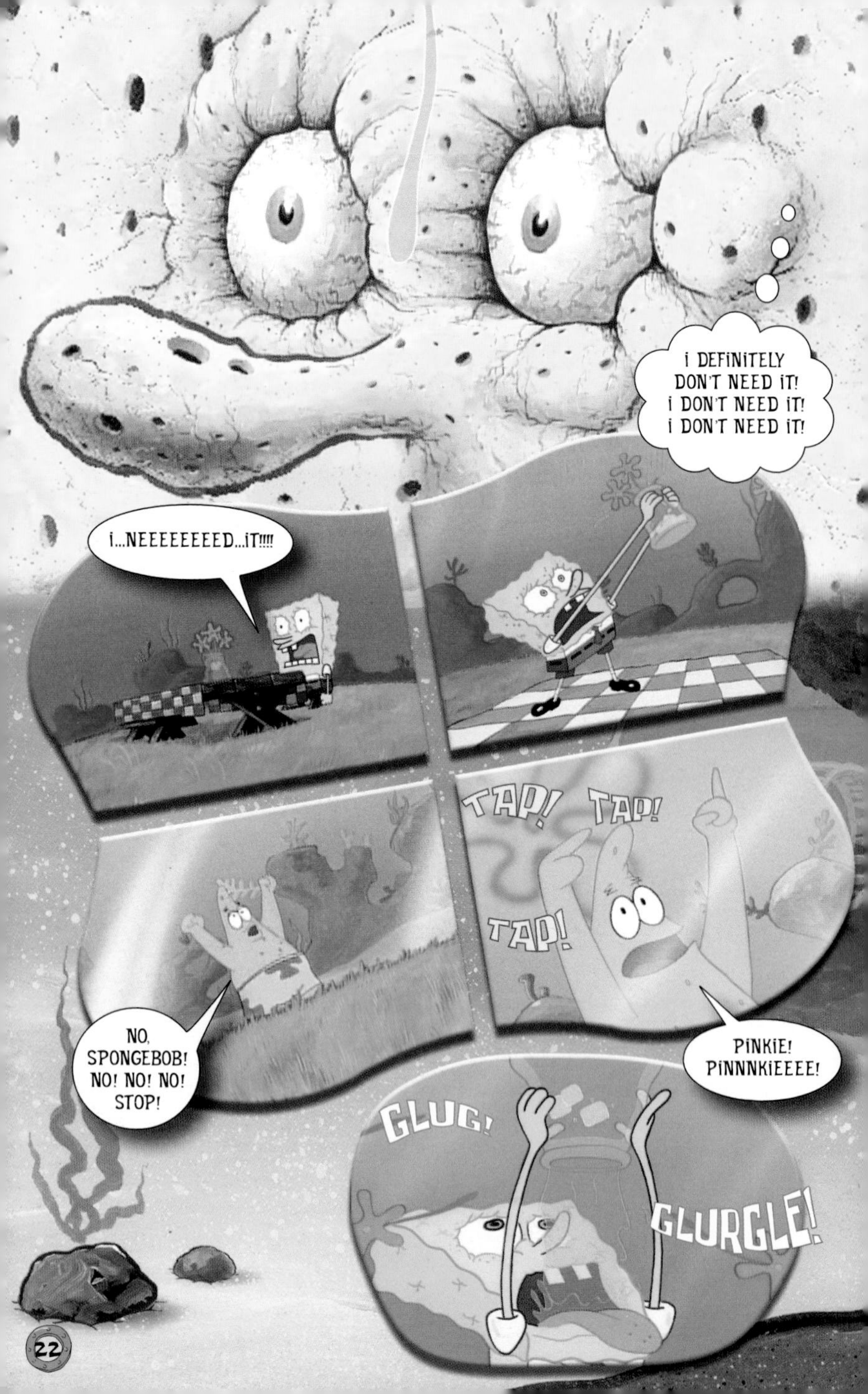

I DEFINITELY DON'T NEED IT! I DON'T NEED IT! I DON'T NEED IT!
I...NEEEEEEEED...IT!!!!
TAP! TAP!
TAP!
NO, SPONGEBOB! NO! NO! NO! STOP!
PINKIE! PINNNKIEEEE!
GLUG!
GLURGLE!

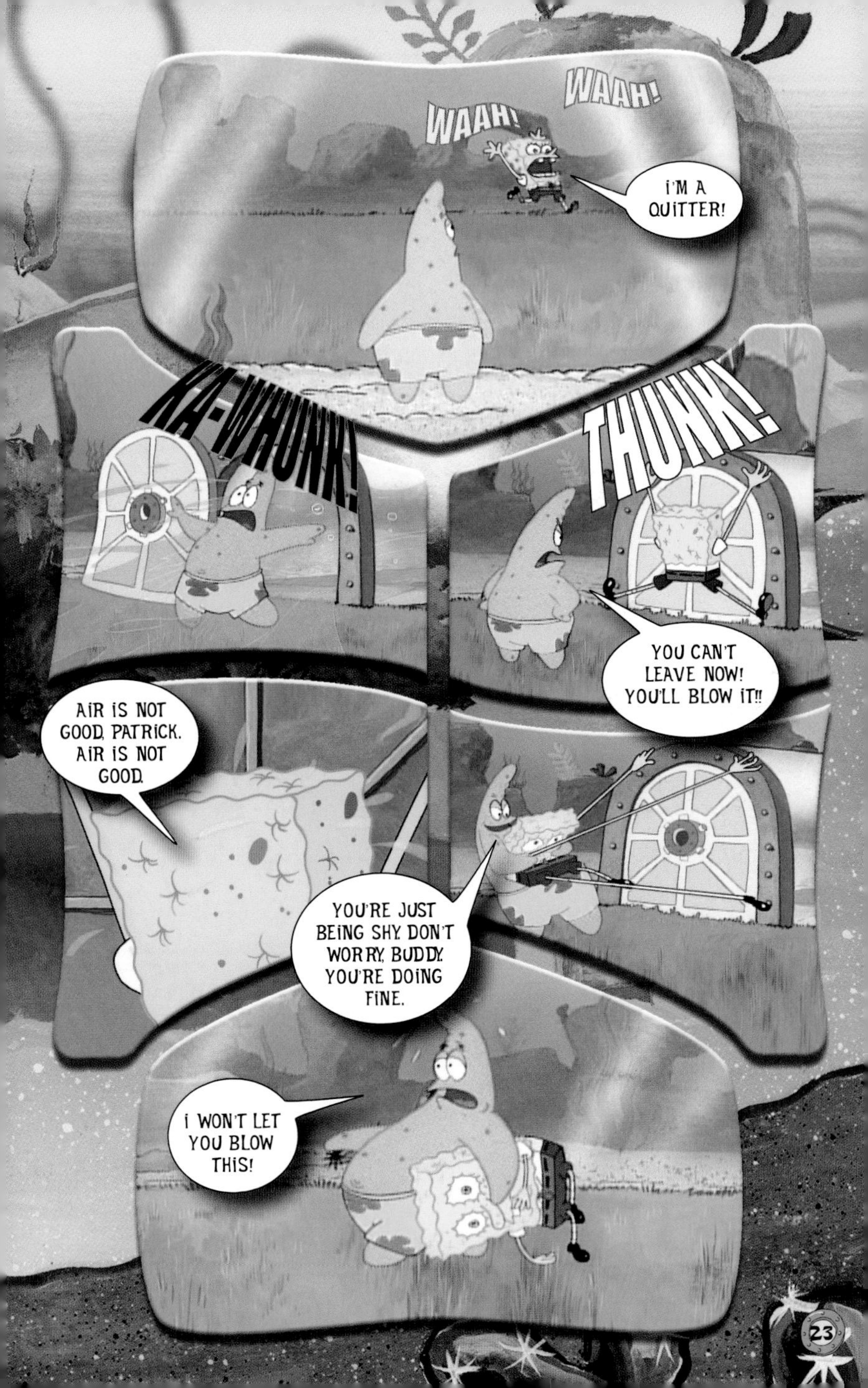
WAAH!
WAAH!
I'M A QUITTER!
KA-WHUNK!
THUNK!
YOU CAN'T LEAVE NOW! YOU'LL BLOW IT!!
AIR IS NOT GOOD, PATRICK. AIR IS NOT GOOD.
YOU'RE JUST BEING SHY. DON'T WORRY, BUDDY. YOU'RE DOING FINE.
I WON'T LET YOU BLOW THIS!

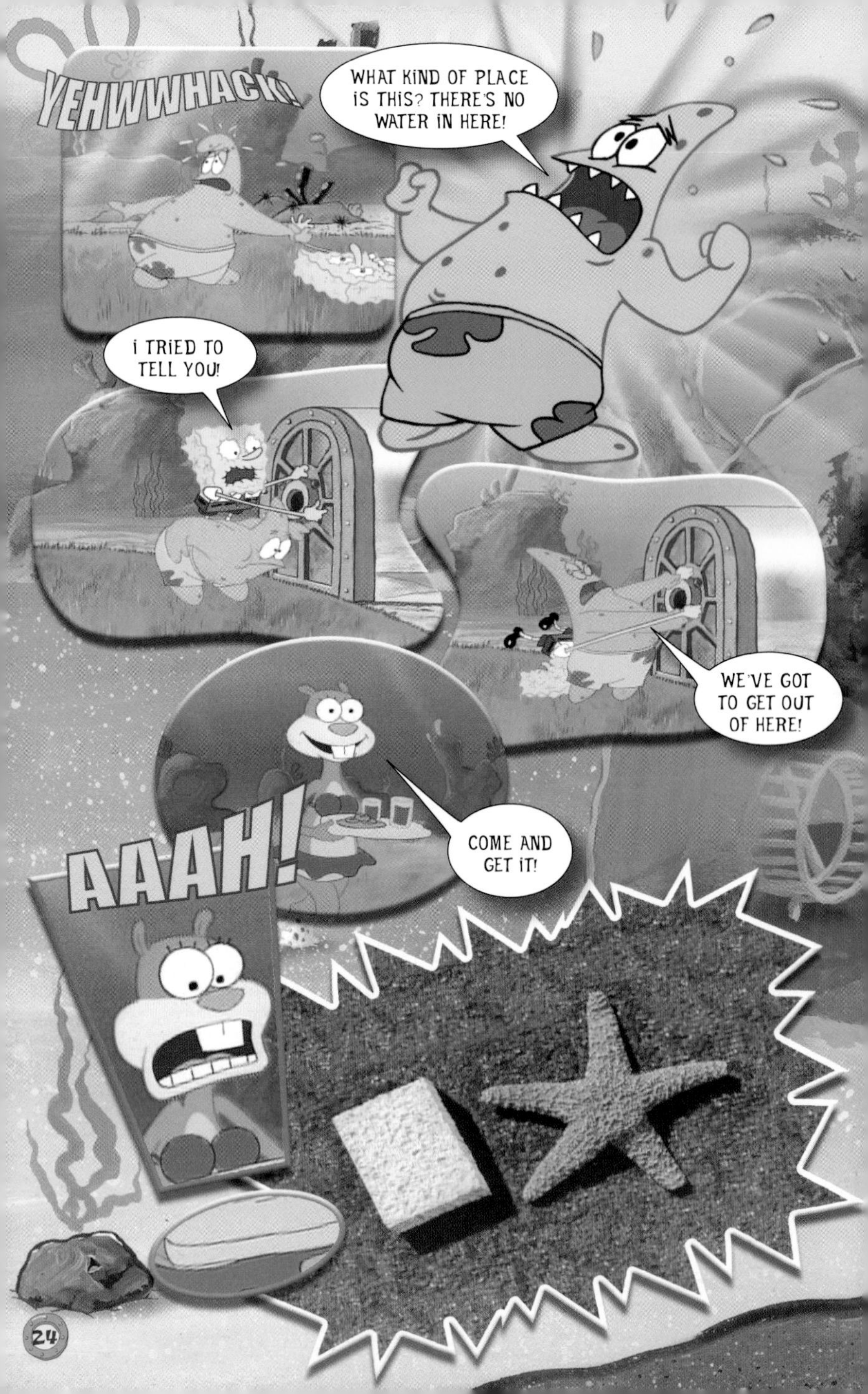
YEHWWHACK!
WHAT KIND OF PLACE IS THIS? THERE'S NO WATER IN HERE!
I TRIED TO TELL YOU!
WE'VE GOT TO GET OUT OF HERE!
COME AND GET IT!
AAAH!

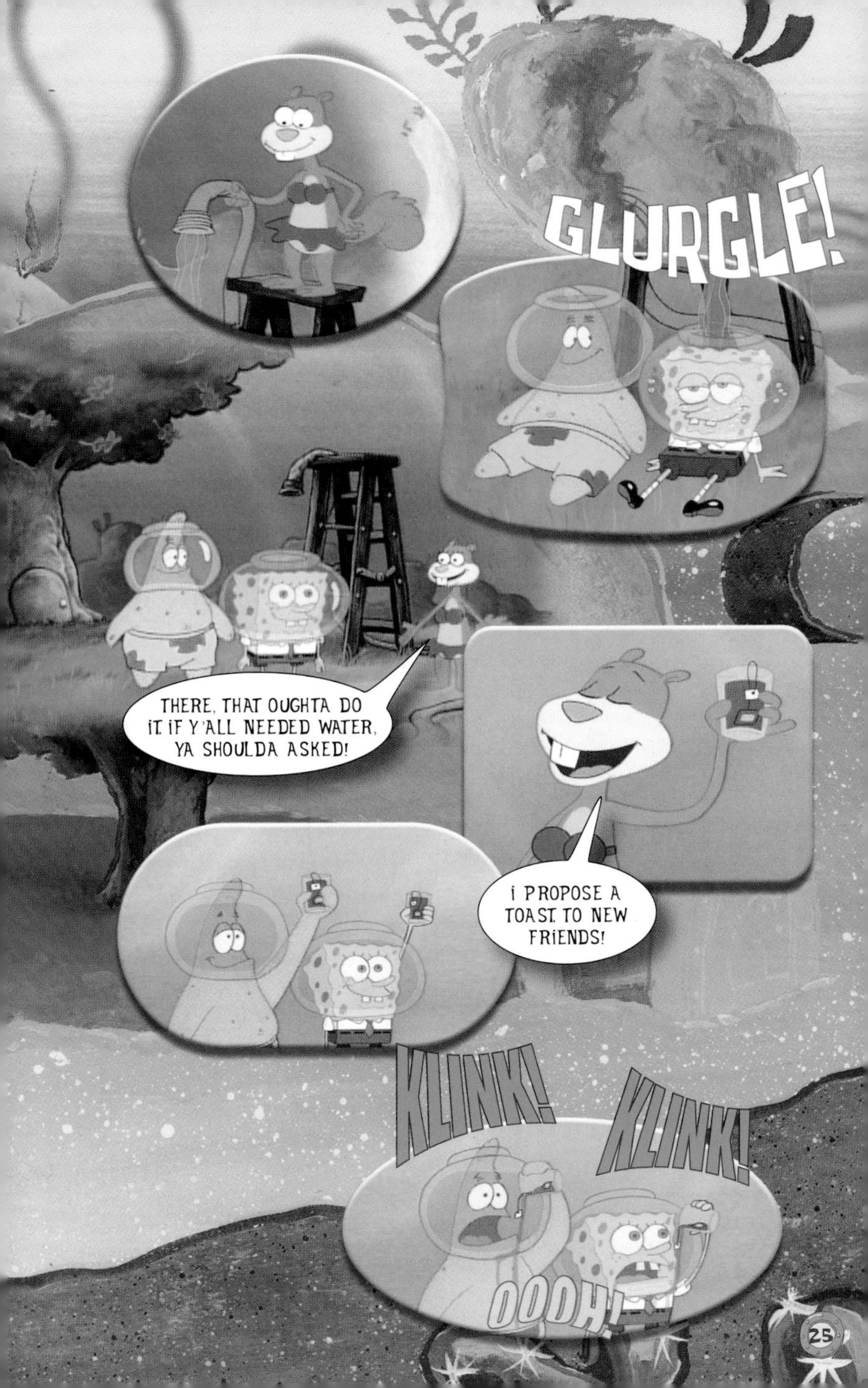
GLURGLE!
THERE, THAT OUGHTA DO IT. IF Y'ALL NEEDED WATER, YA SHOULDA ASKED!
I PROPOSE A TOAST. TO NEW FRIENDS!
KLINK!
KLINK!
OOOH!

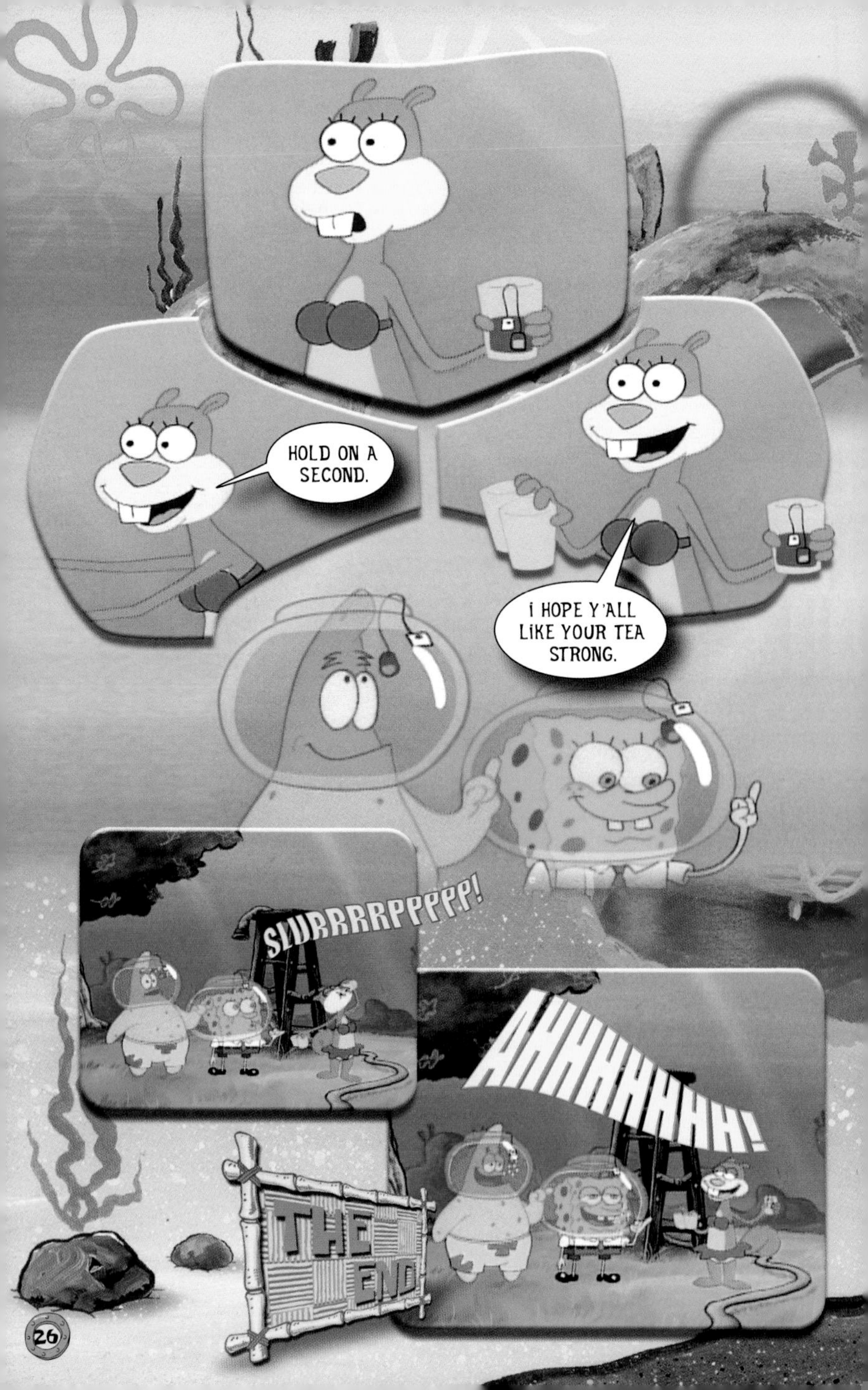
HOLD ON A SECOND.
I HOPE Y'ALL LIKE YOUR TEA STRONG.
SLURRRRPPPPP!
AHHHHHHH!
THE END

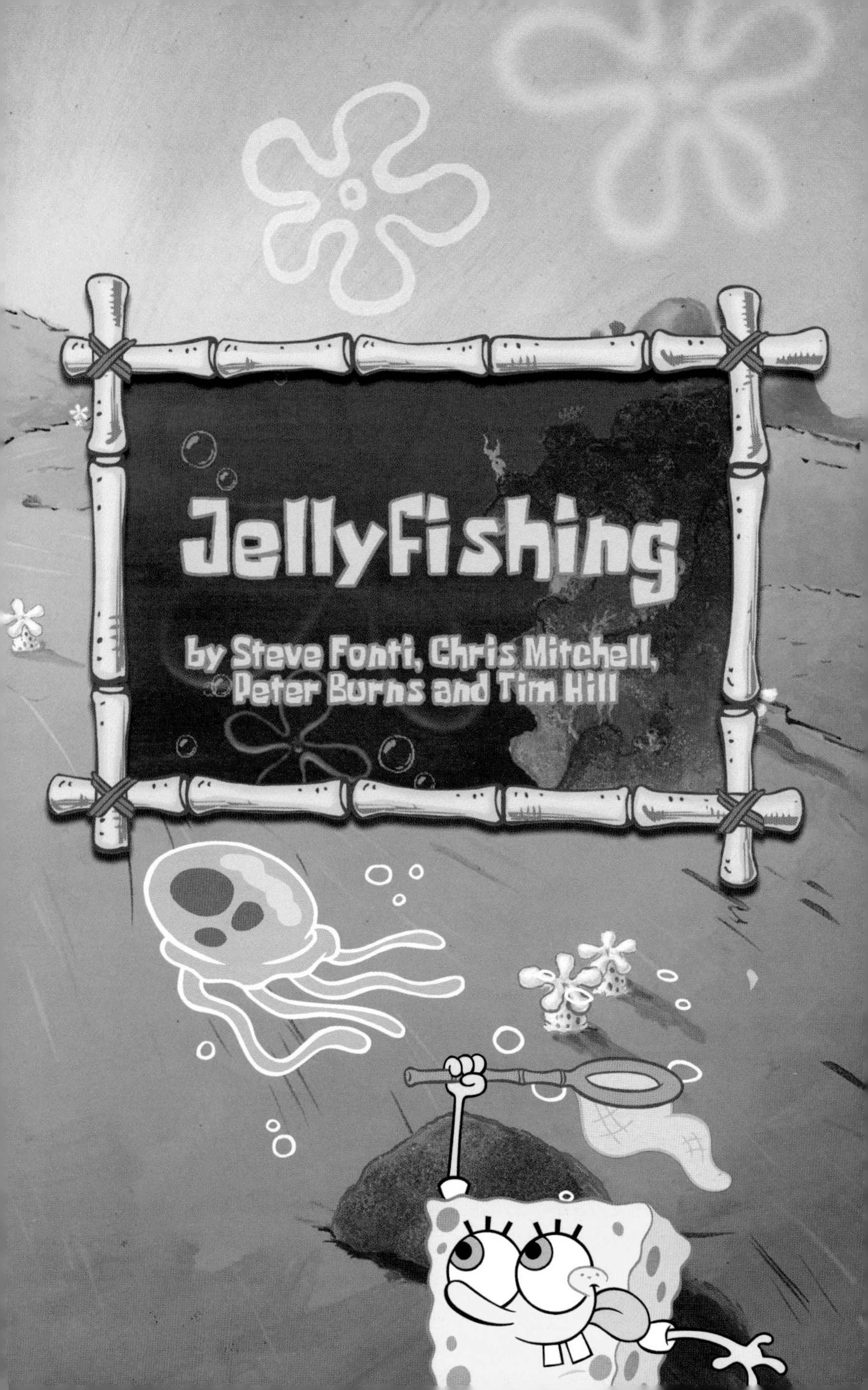
Jellyfishing
by Steve Fonti, Chris Mitchell, Peter Burns and Tim Hill

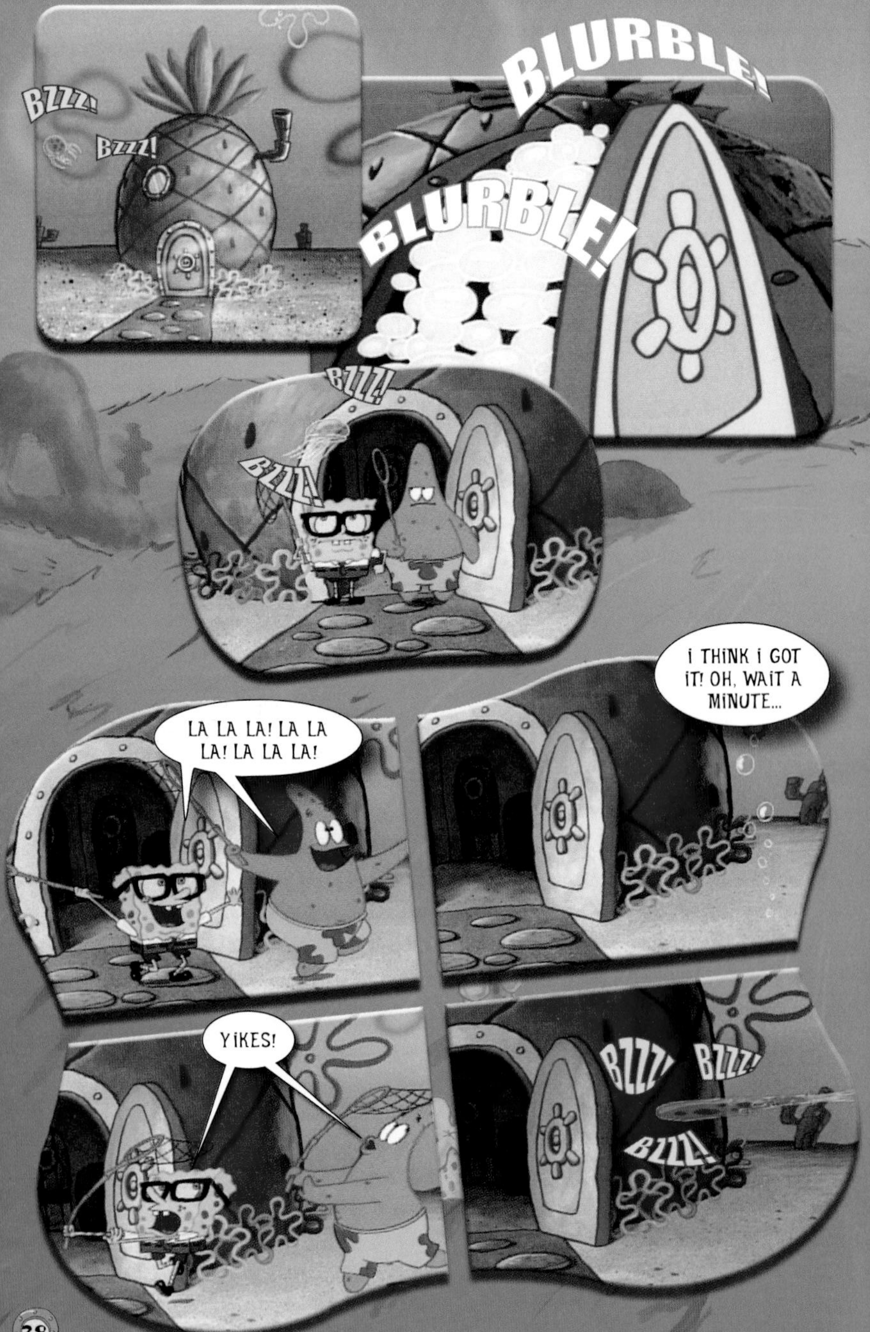
BZZZ!
BZZZ!
BLURBLE!
BLURBLE!
BZZZ!
BZZZ!
LA LA LA! LA LA LA! LA LA LA!
I THINK I GOT IT! OH, WAIT A MINUTE...
YIKES!
BZZZ!
BZZZ!
BZZZ!

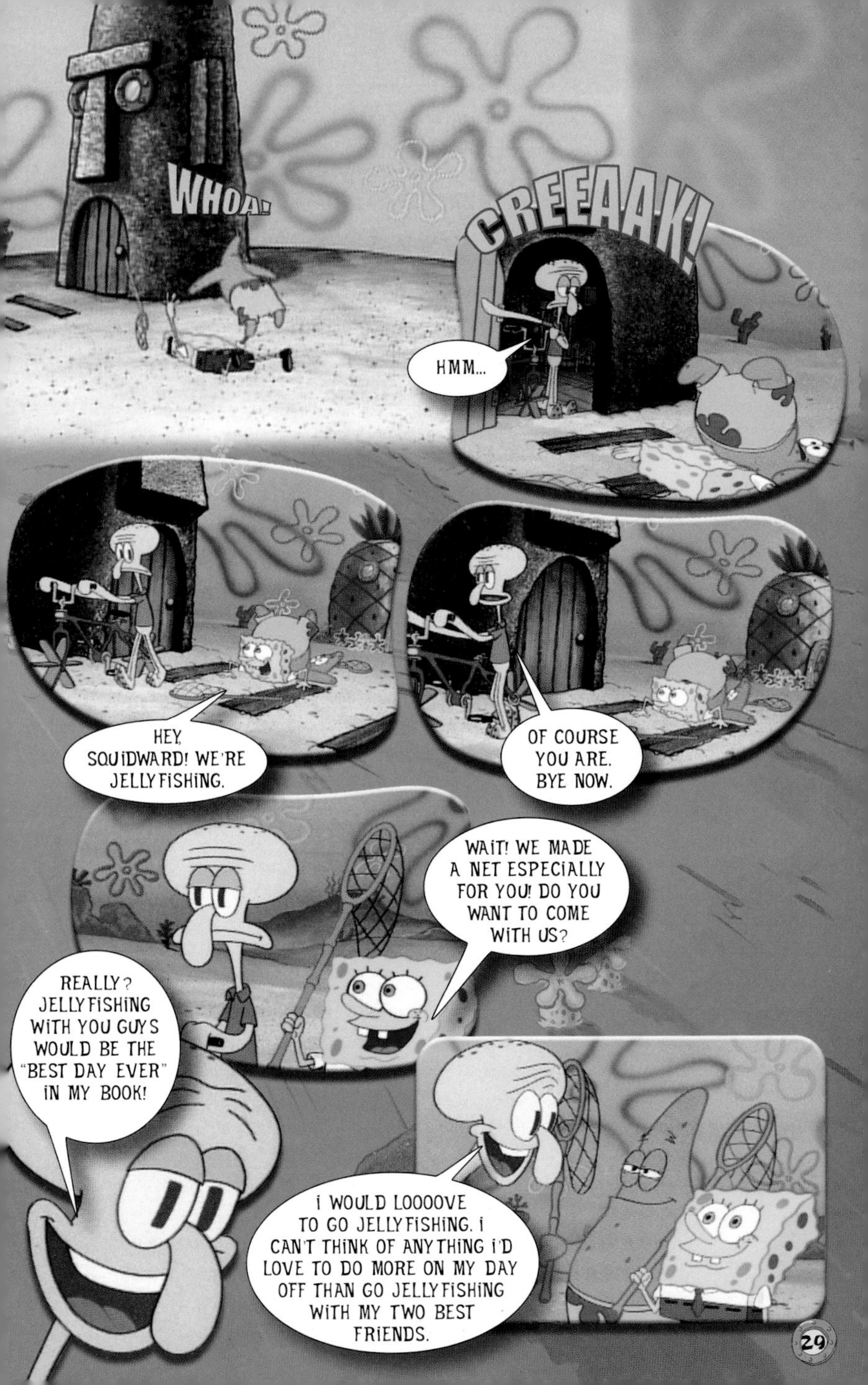
WHOA!
CREEAAK!
HMM...
HEY, SQUIDWARD! WE'RE JELLYFISHING.
OF COURSE YOU ARE. BYE NOW.
WAIT! WE MADE A NET ESPECIALLY FOR YOU! DO YOU WANT TO COME WITH US?
REALLY? JELLYFISHING WITH YOU GUYS WOULD BE THE "BEST DAY EVER" IN MY BOOK!
I WOULD LOOOOVE TO GO JELLYFISHING. I CAN'T THINK OF ANYTHING I'D LOVE TO DO MORE ON MY DAY OFF THAN GO JELLYFISHING WITH MY TWO BEST FRIENDS.

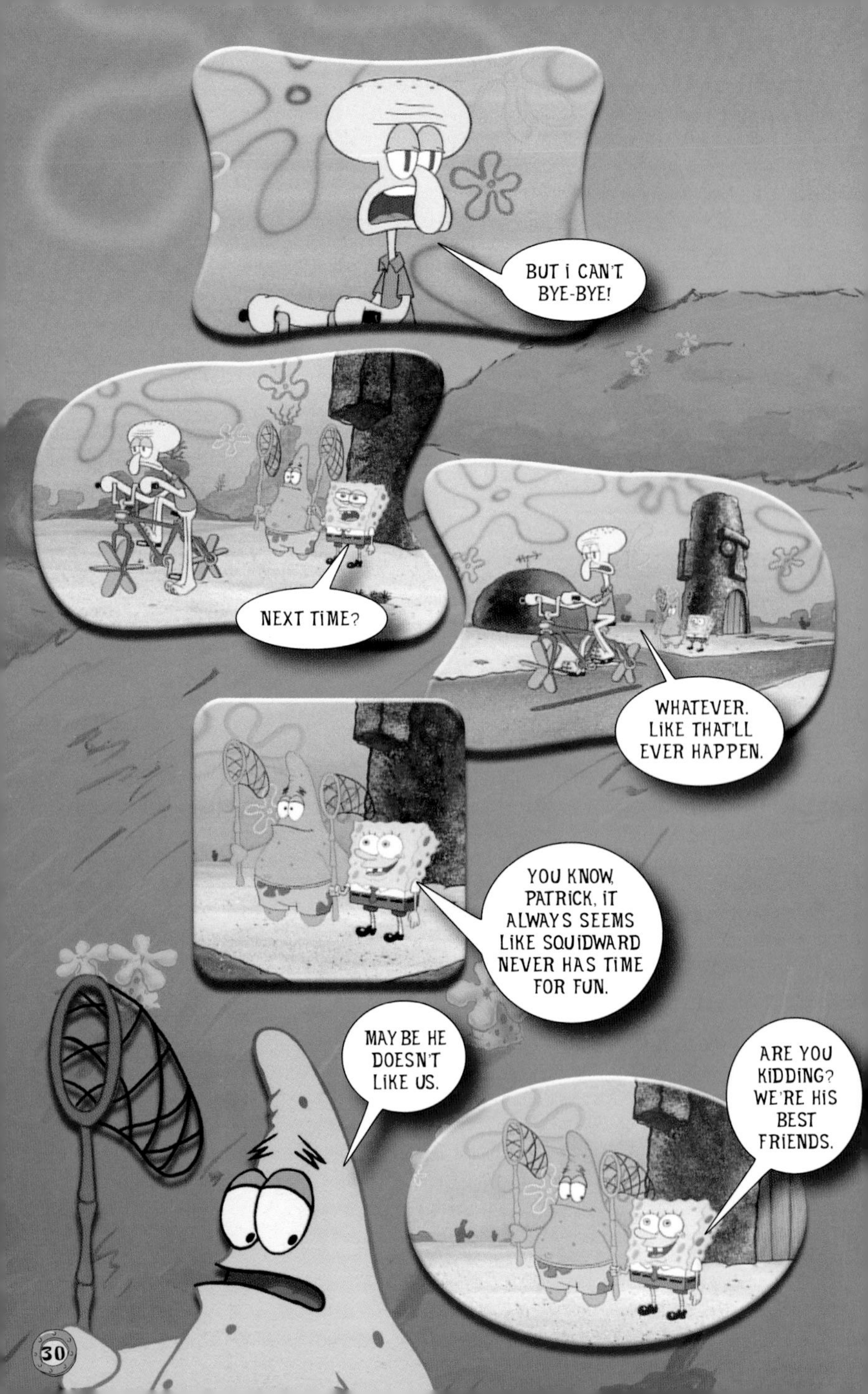
BUT I CAN'T. BYE-BYE!
NEXT TIME?
WHATEVER. LIKE THAT'LL EVER HAPPEN.
YOU KNOW, PATRICK, IT ALWAYS SEEMS LIKE SQUIDWARD NEVER HAS TIME FOR FUN.
MAYBE HE DOESN'T LIKE US.
ARE YOU KIDDING? WE'RE HIS BEST FRIENDS.

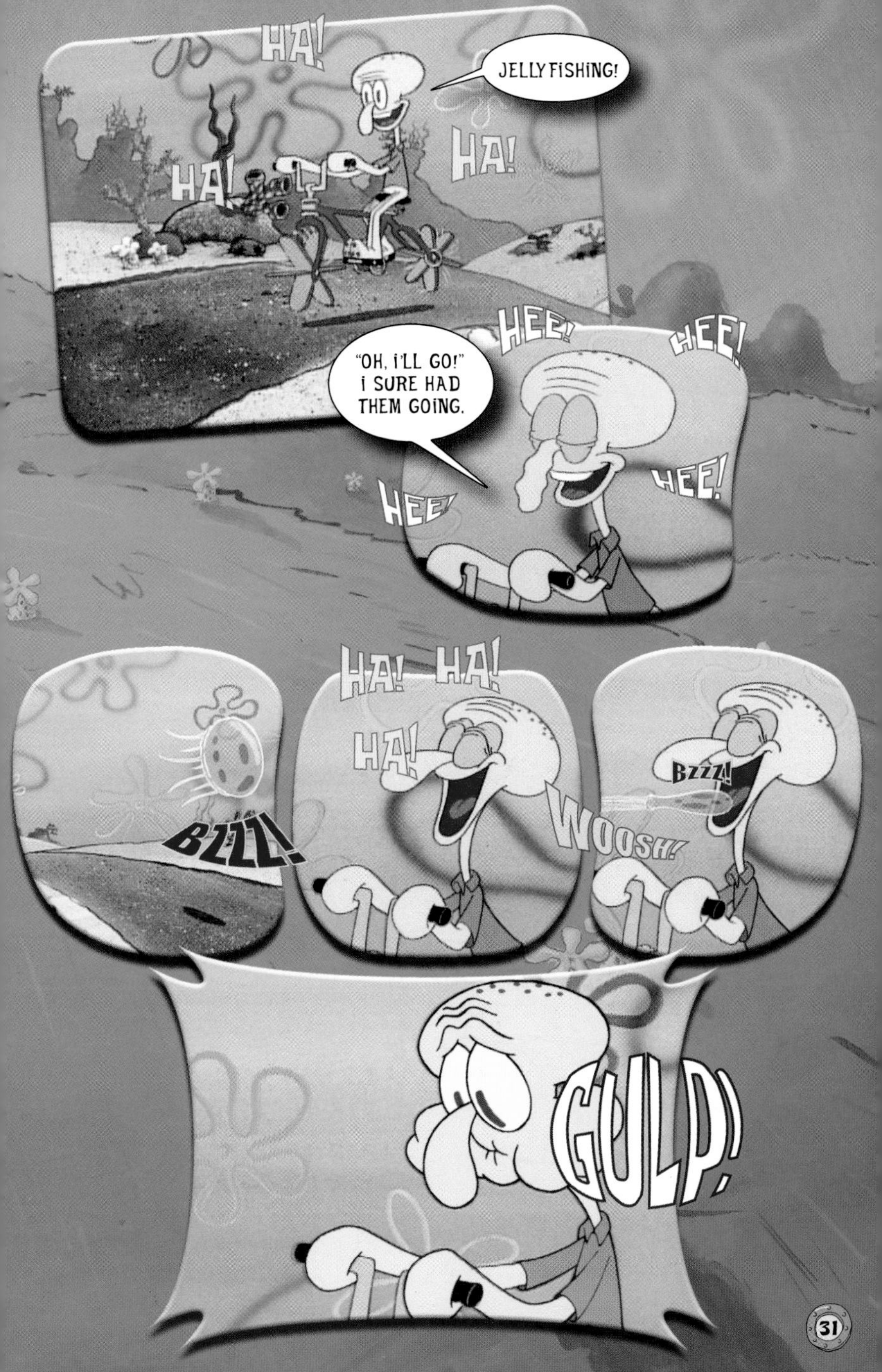

HA!
JELLYFISHING!
HA!
HA!
HEE!
HEE!
"OH, I'LL GO!" I SURE HAD THEM GOING.
HEE!
HEE!
BZZZ!
HA! HA!
HA!
WOOSH!
BZZZ!
GULP!

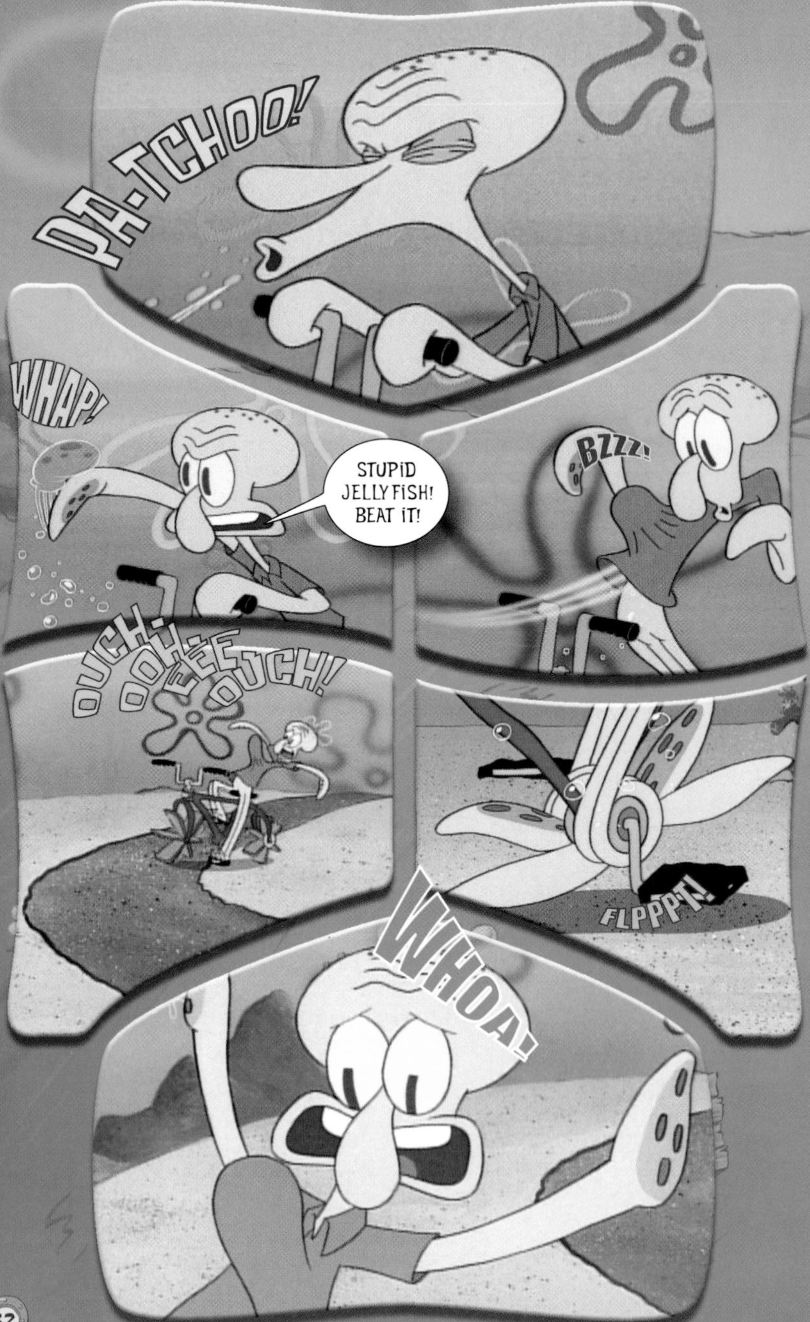

AH-TCHOO!
WHAP!
STUPID JELLYFISH! BEAT IT!
BZZZ!
OUCH-OOH-EEE-OUCH!
FLPPPT!
WHOA!

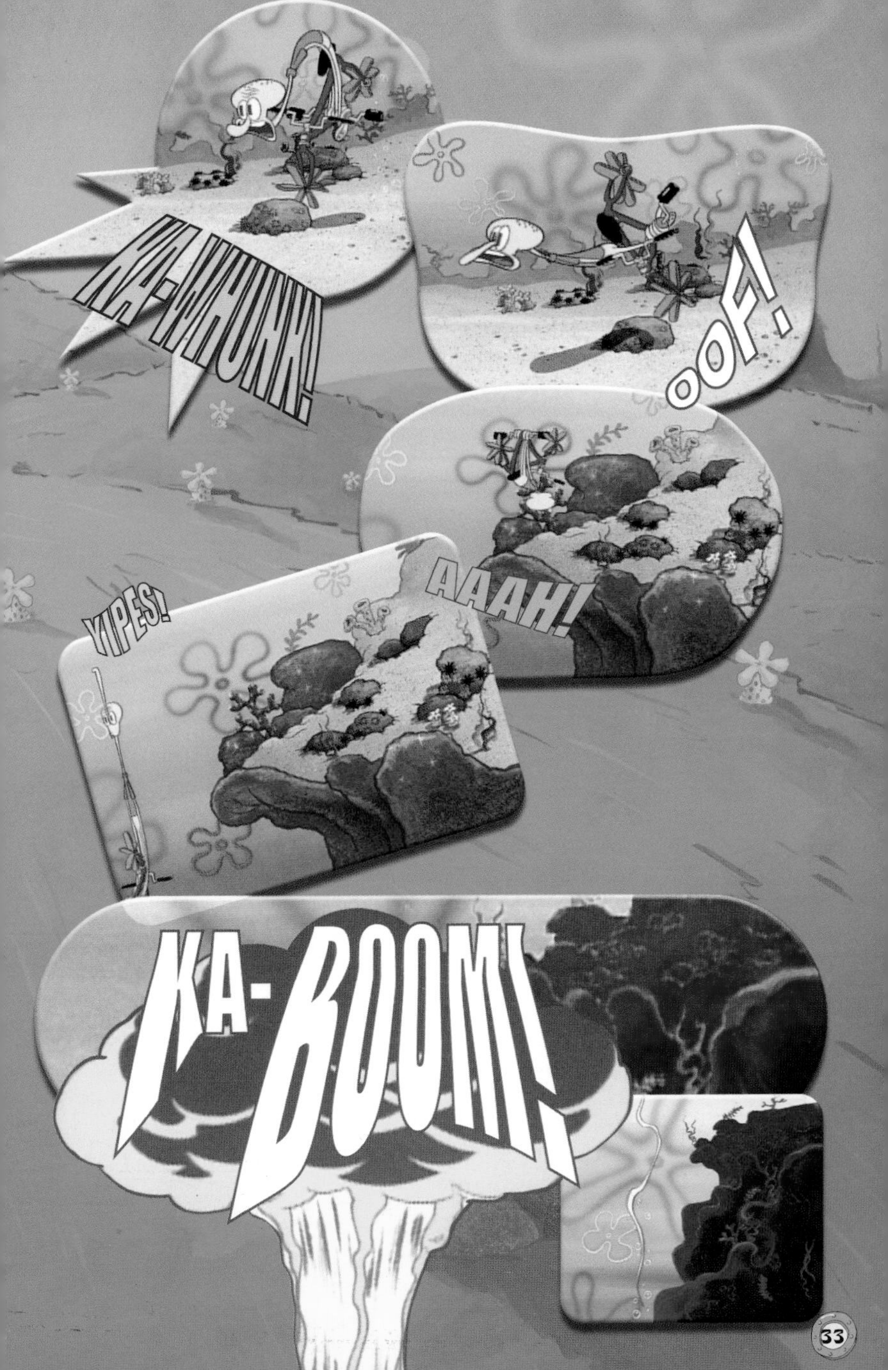
KA-WHUNK!
OOF!
AAAH!
YIPES!
KA-BOOM!

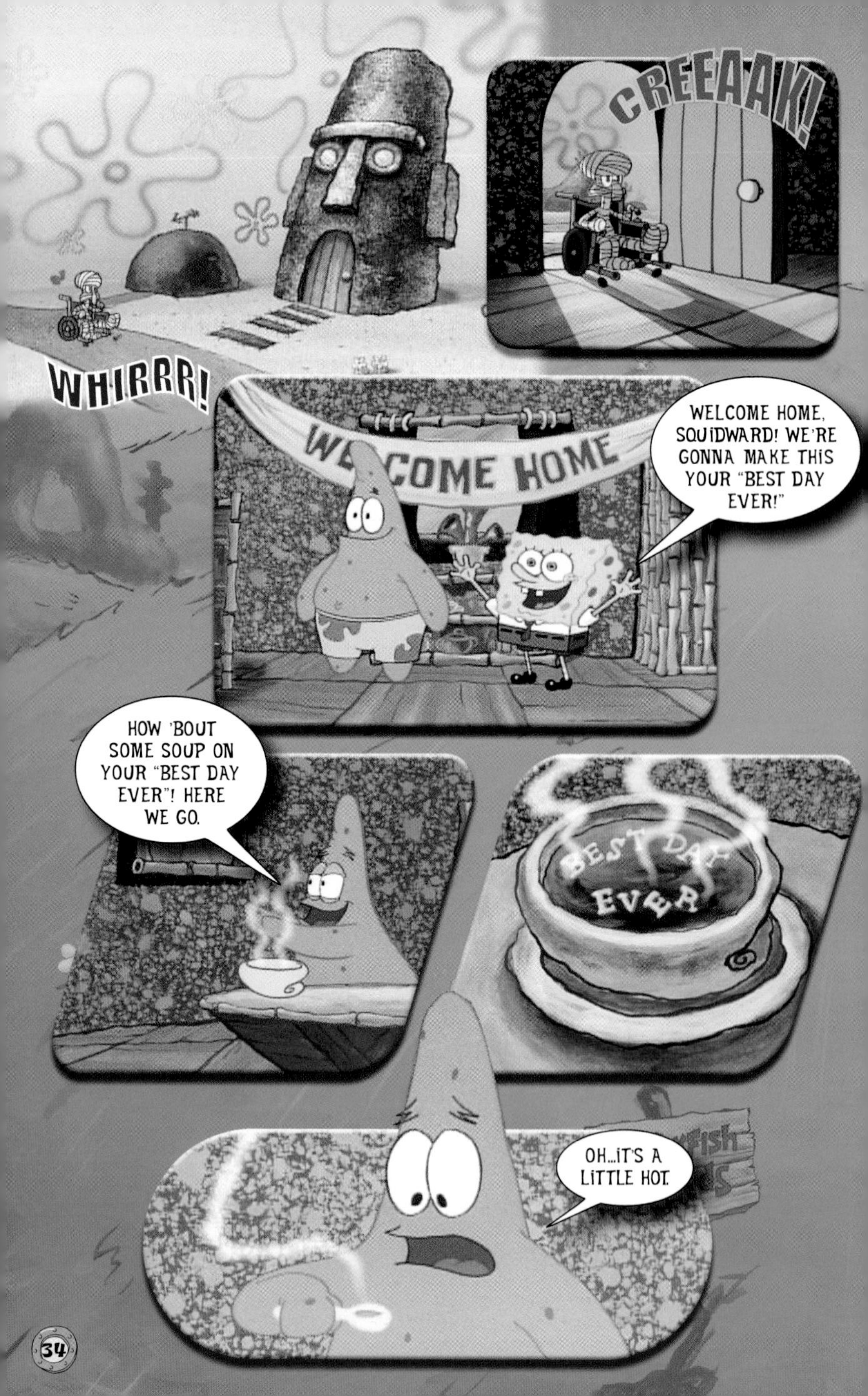
WHIRRR!
CREEAAK!
WELCOME HOME
WELCOME HOME, SQUIDWARD! WE'RE GONNA MAKE THIS YOUR "BEST DAY EVER!"
HOW 'BOUT SOME SOUP ON YOUR "BEST DAY EVER"! HERE WE GO.
BEST DAY EVER
OH...IT'S A LITTLE HOT.

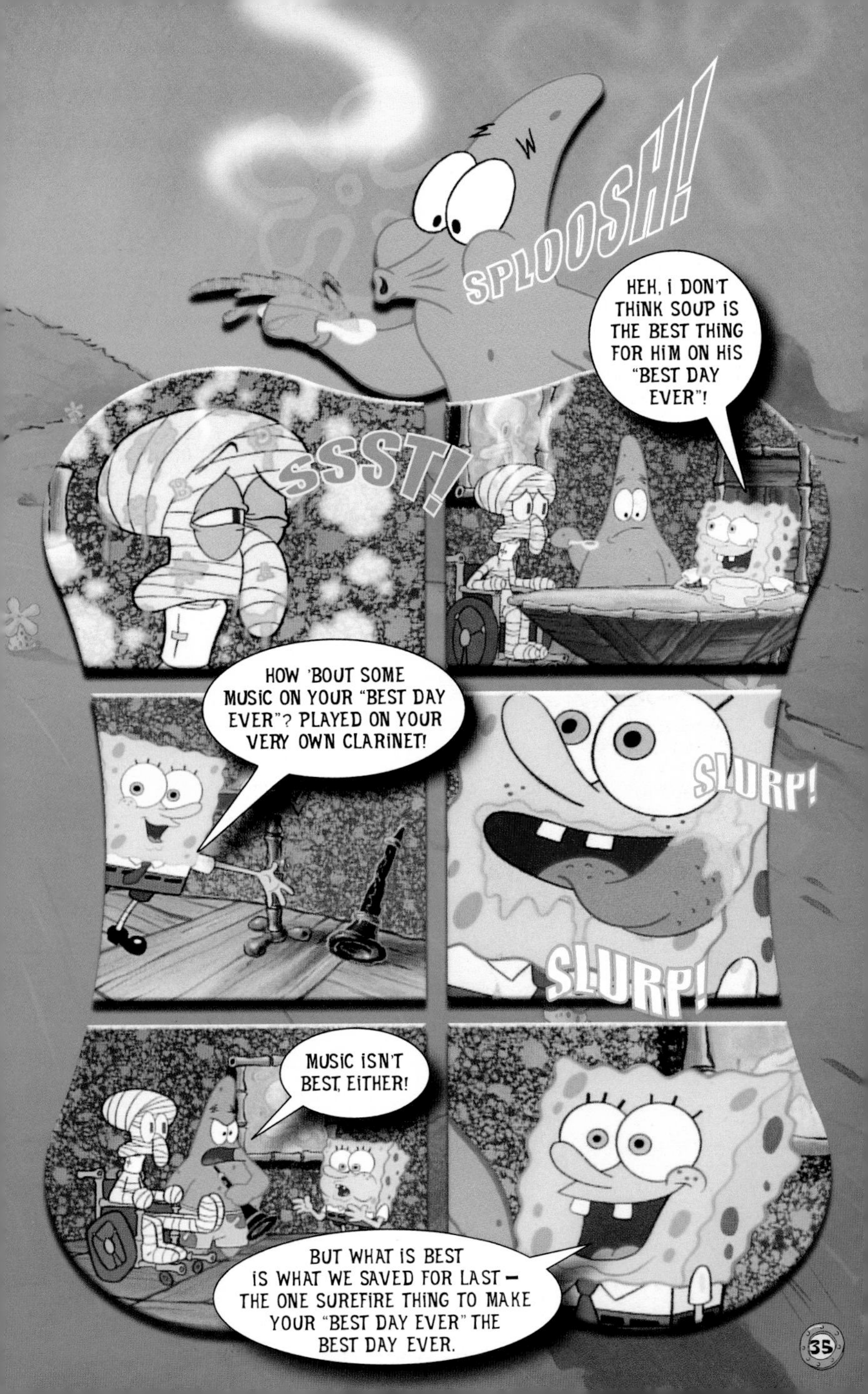
SPLOOSH!
HEH, I DON'T THINK SOUP IS THE BEST THING FOR HIM ON HIS "BEST DAY EVER"!
SSST!
HOW 'BOUT SOME MUSIC ON YOUR "BEST DAY EVER"? PLAYED ON YOUR VERY OWN CLARINET!
SLURP!
SLURP!
MUSIC ISN'T BEST, EITHER!
BUT WHAT IS BEST IS WHAT WE SAVED FOR LAST — THE ONE SUREFIRE THING TO MAKE YOUR "BEST DAY EVER" THE BEST DAY EVER.

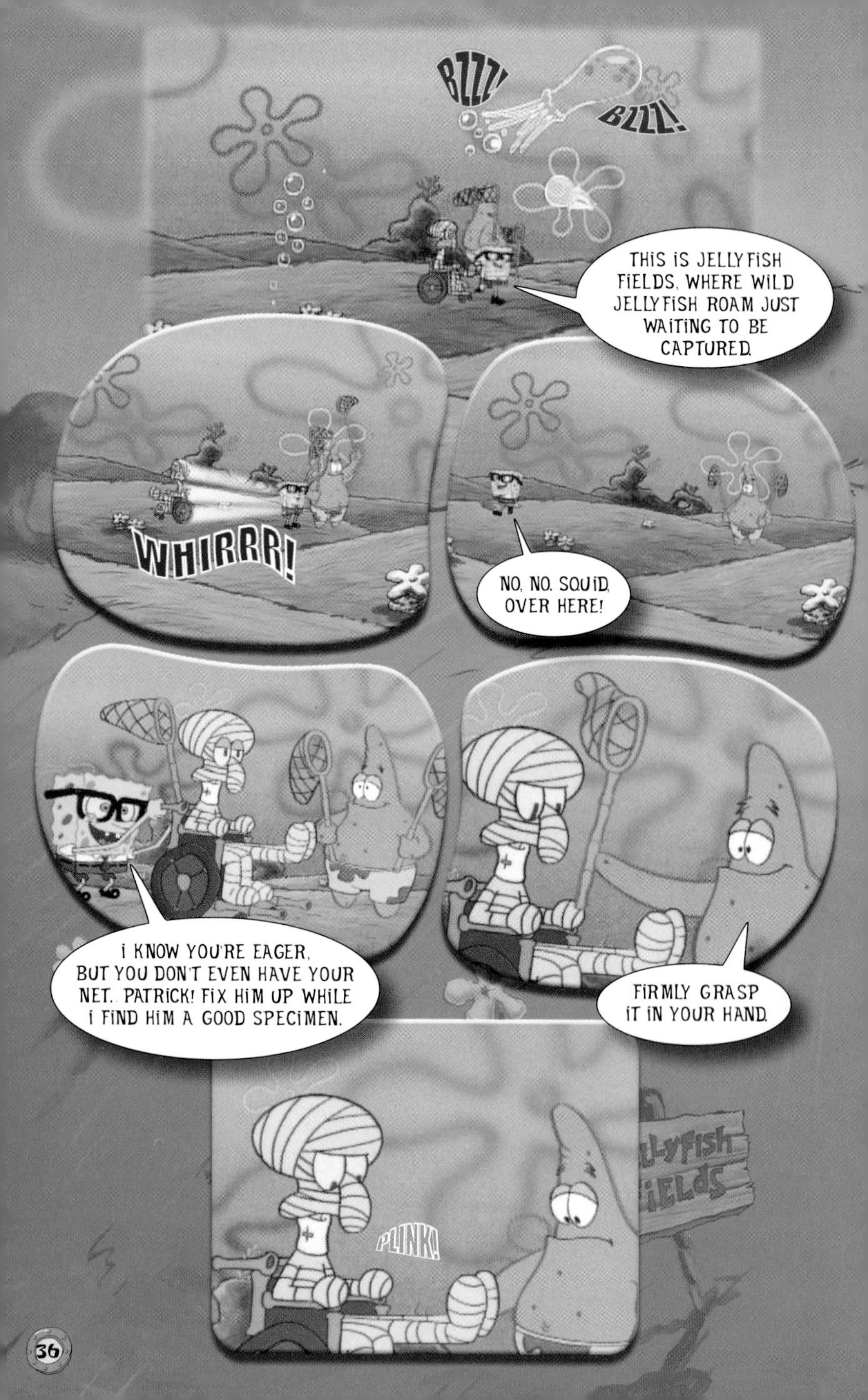
BZZZ!
BZZZ!
THIS IS JELLYFISH FIELDS, WHERE WILD JELLYFISH ROAM JUST WAITING TO BE CAPTURED.
WHIRRR!
NO, NO. SQUID, OVER HERE!
I KNOW YOU'RE EAGER, BUT YOU DON'T EVEN HAVE YOUR NET.. PATRICK! FIX HIM UP WHILE I FIND HIM A GOOD SPECIMEN.
FIRMLY GRASP IT IN YOUR HAND.
PLINK!

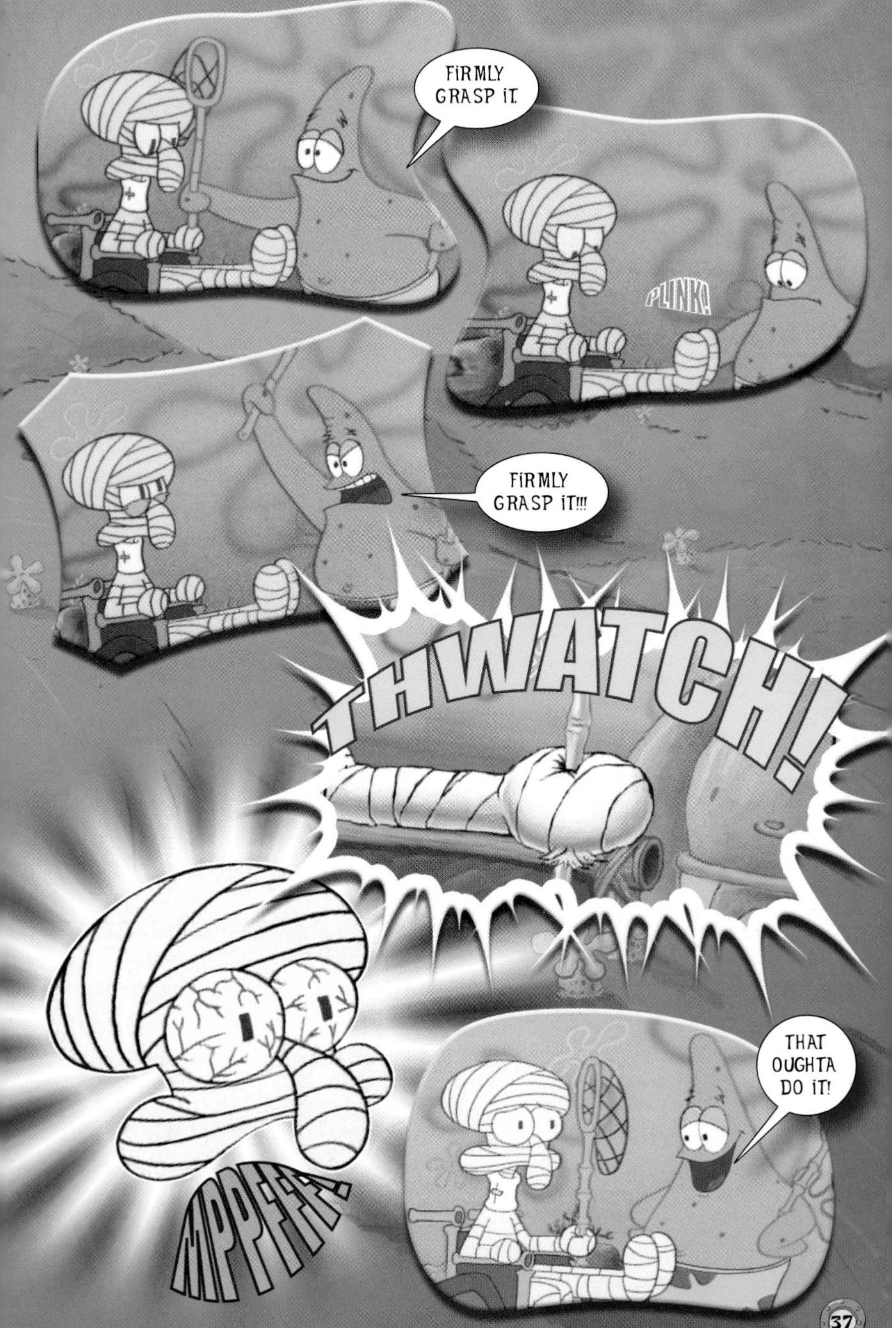
FIRMLY GRASP IT.
PLINK!
FIRMLY GRASP IT!!!
THWATCH!
MPPFFF!
THAT OUGHTA DO IT!

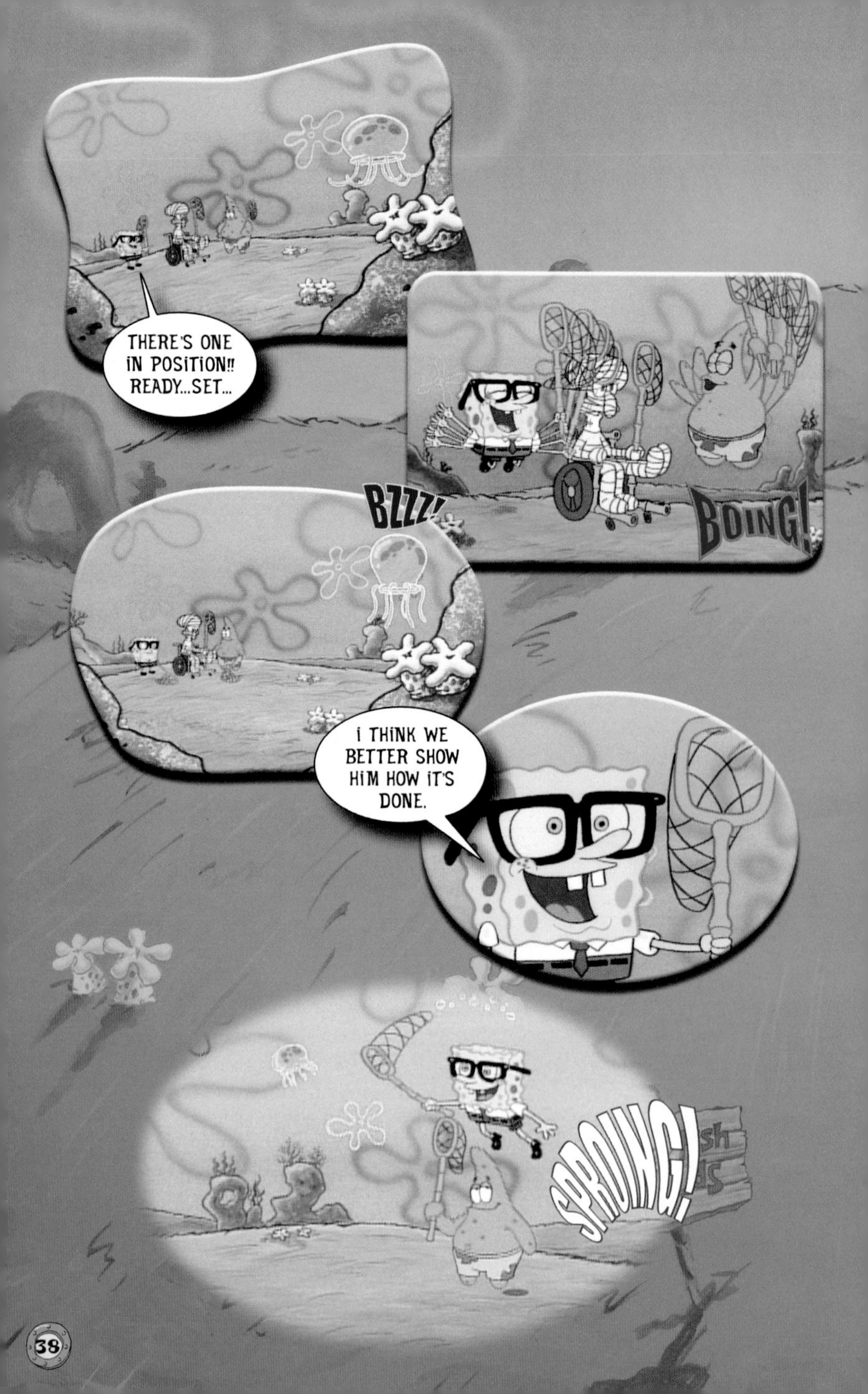
THERE'S ONE IN POSITION!! READY...SET...
BOING!
BZZZ!
I THINK WE BETTER SHOW HIM HOW IT'S DONE.
SPRUNG!

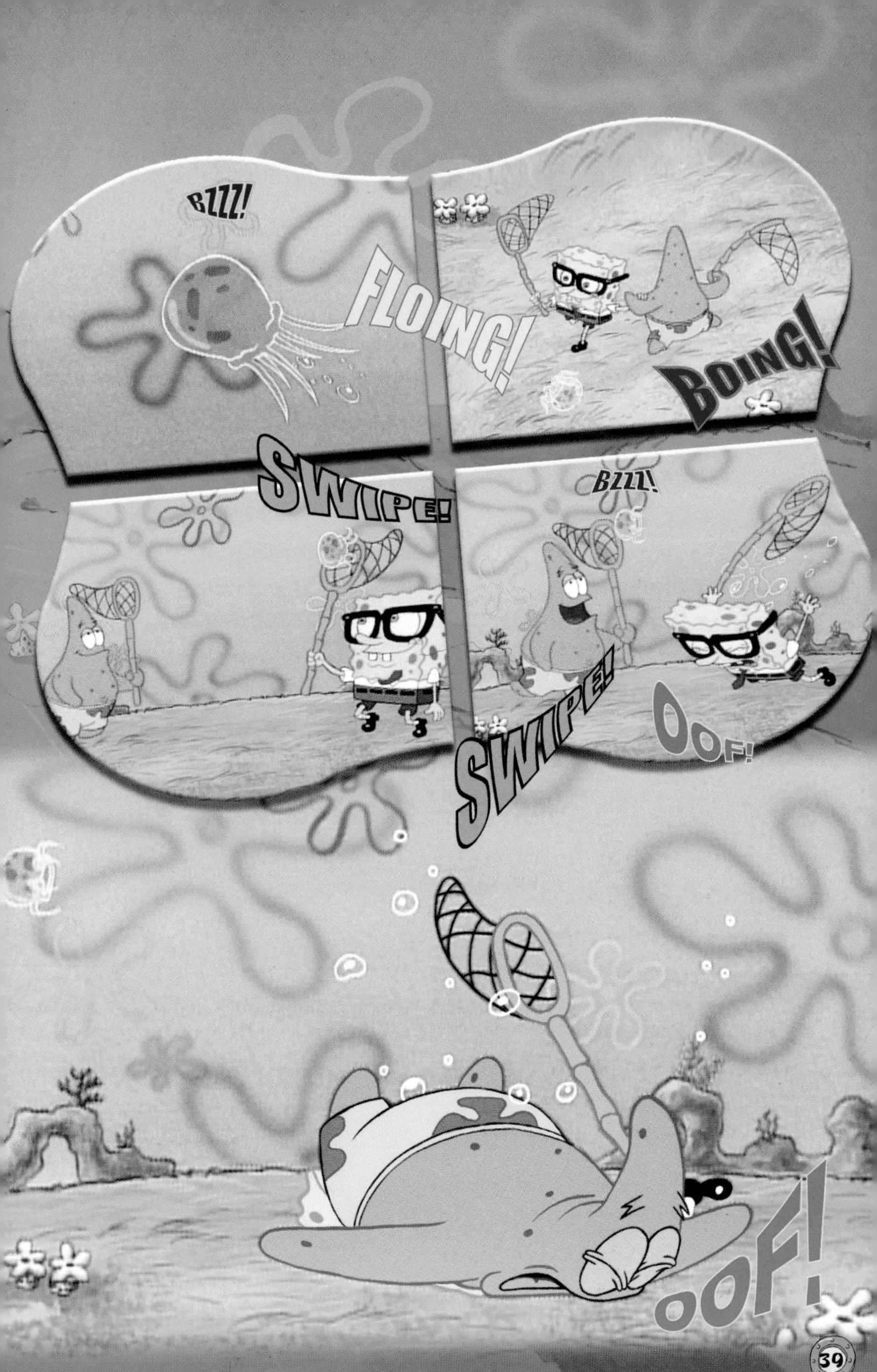
BZZZ!
FLOING!
BOING!
SWIPE!
BZZZ!
SWIPE!
OOF!
OOF!

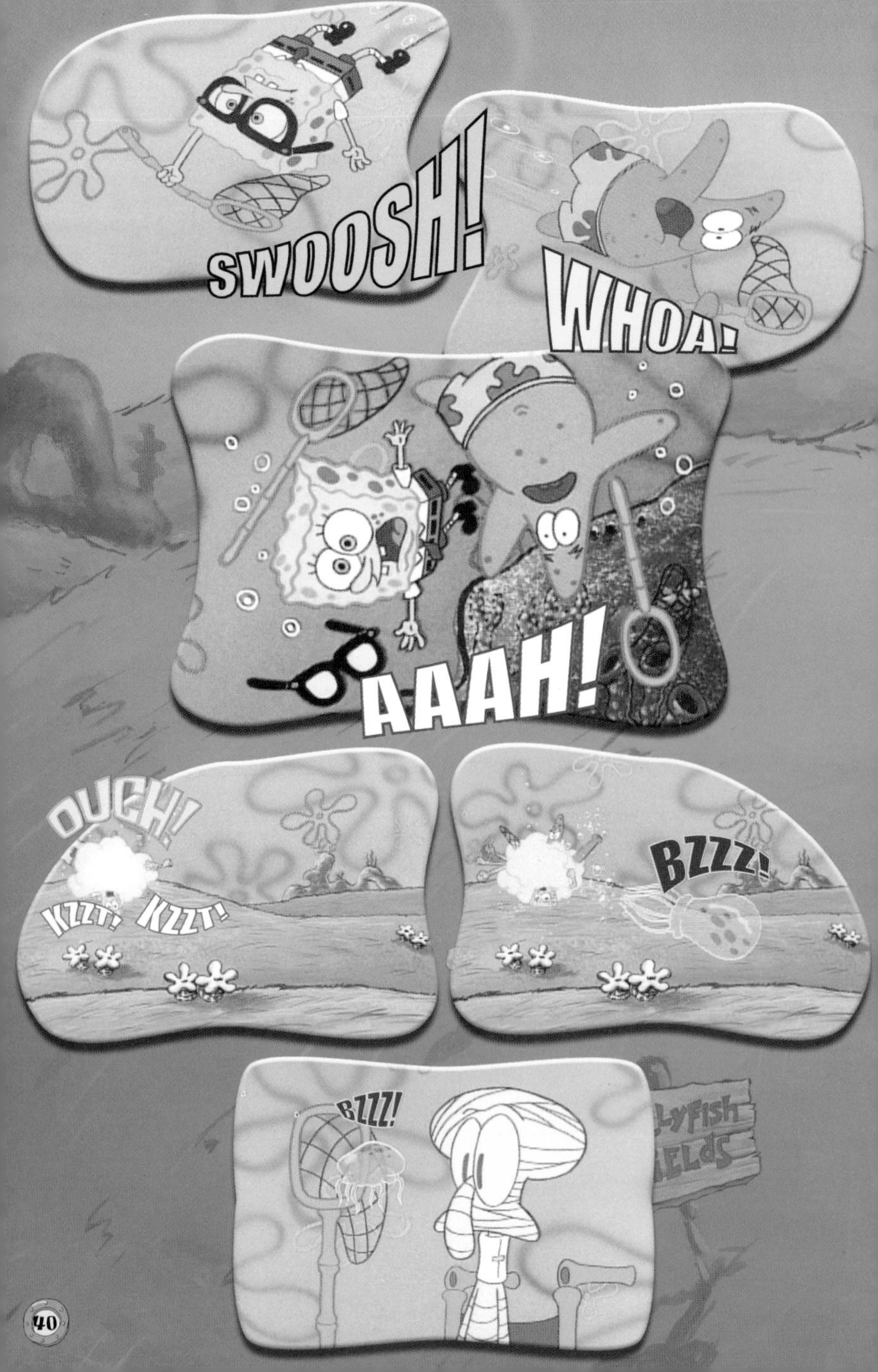
SWOOSH!
WHOA!
AAAH!
OUCH!
KZZT!
KZZT!
BZZZ!
BZZZ!

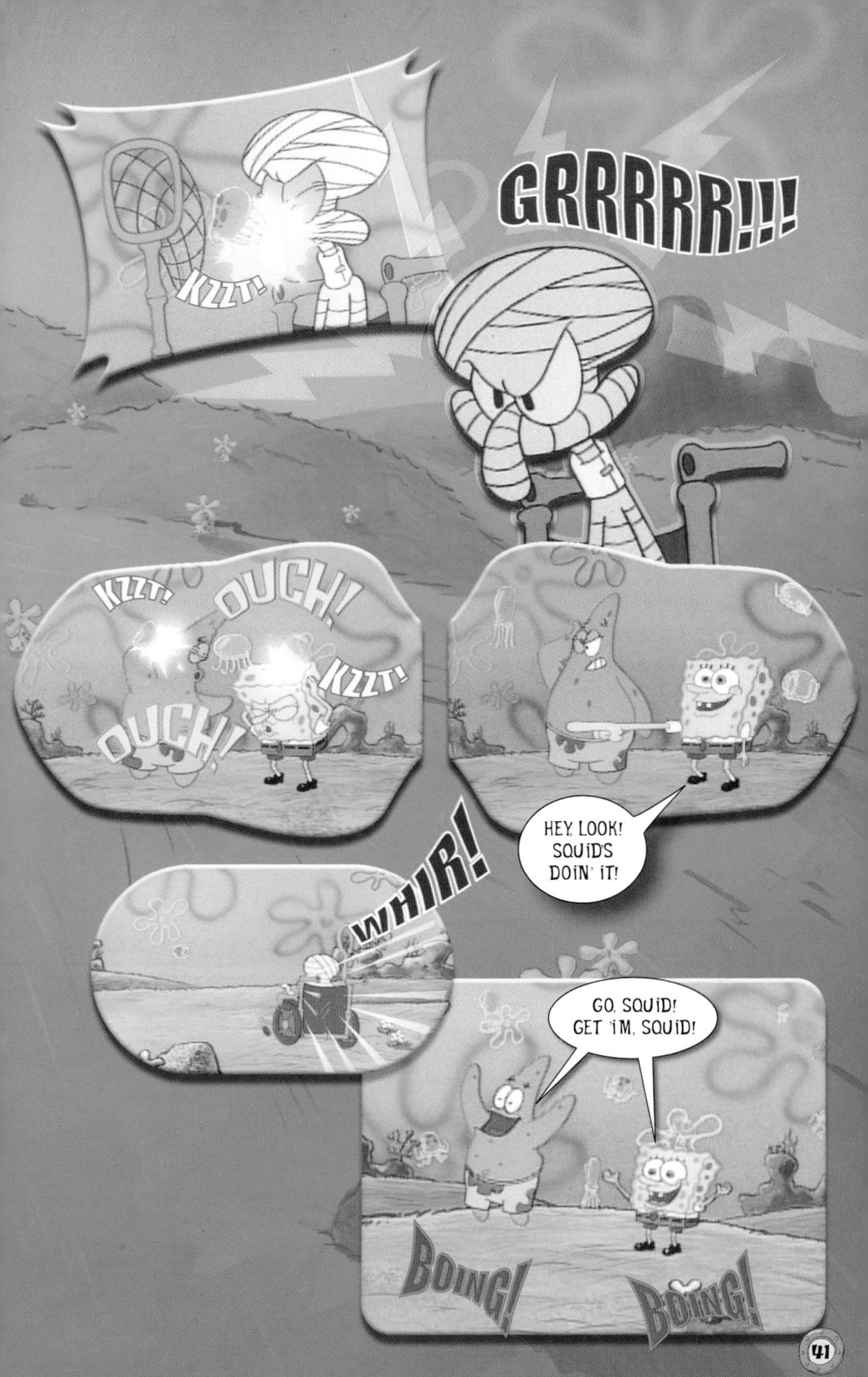
KZZT!
GRRRRRR!!!
KZZT!
OUCH!
KZZT!
OUCH!
HEY, LOOK! SQUID'S DOIN' IT!
WHIR!
GO, SQUID! GET 'IM, SQUID!
BOING!
BOING!

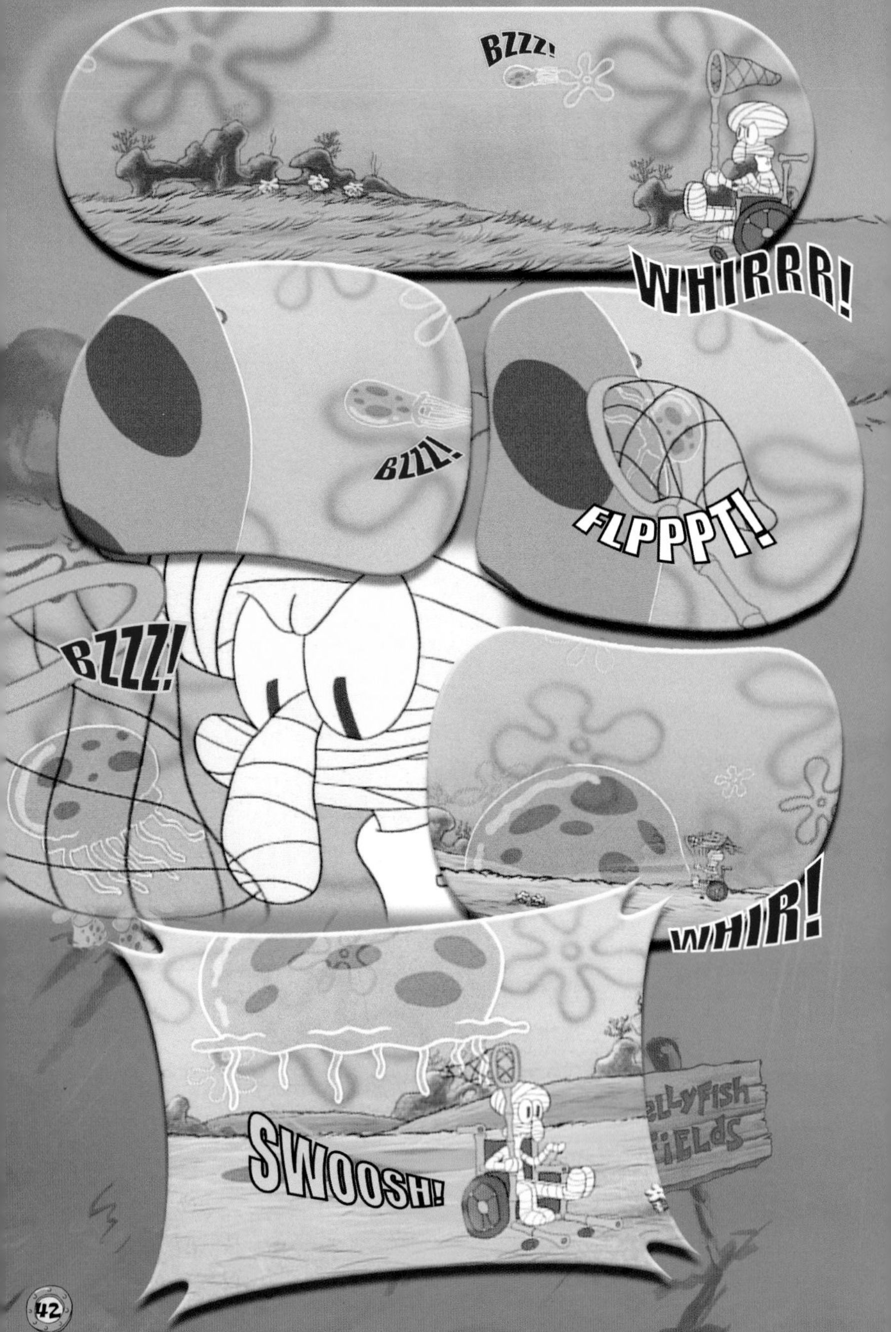
BZZZ!
WHIRRR!
BZZZ!
FLPPPT!
BZZZ!
WHIR!
SWOOSH!
JELLYFISH FIELDS

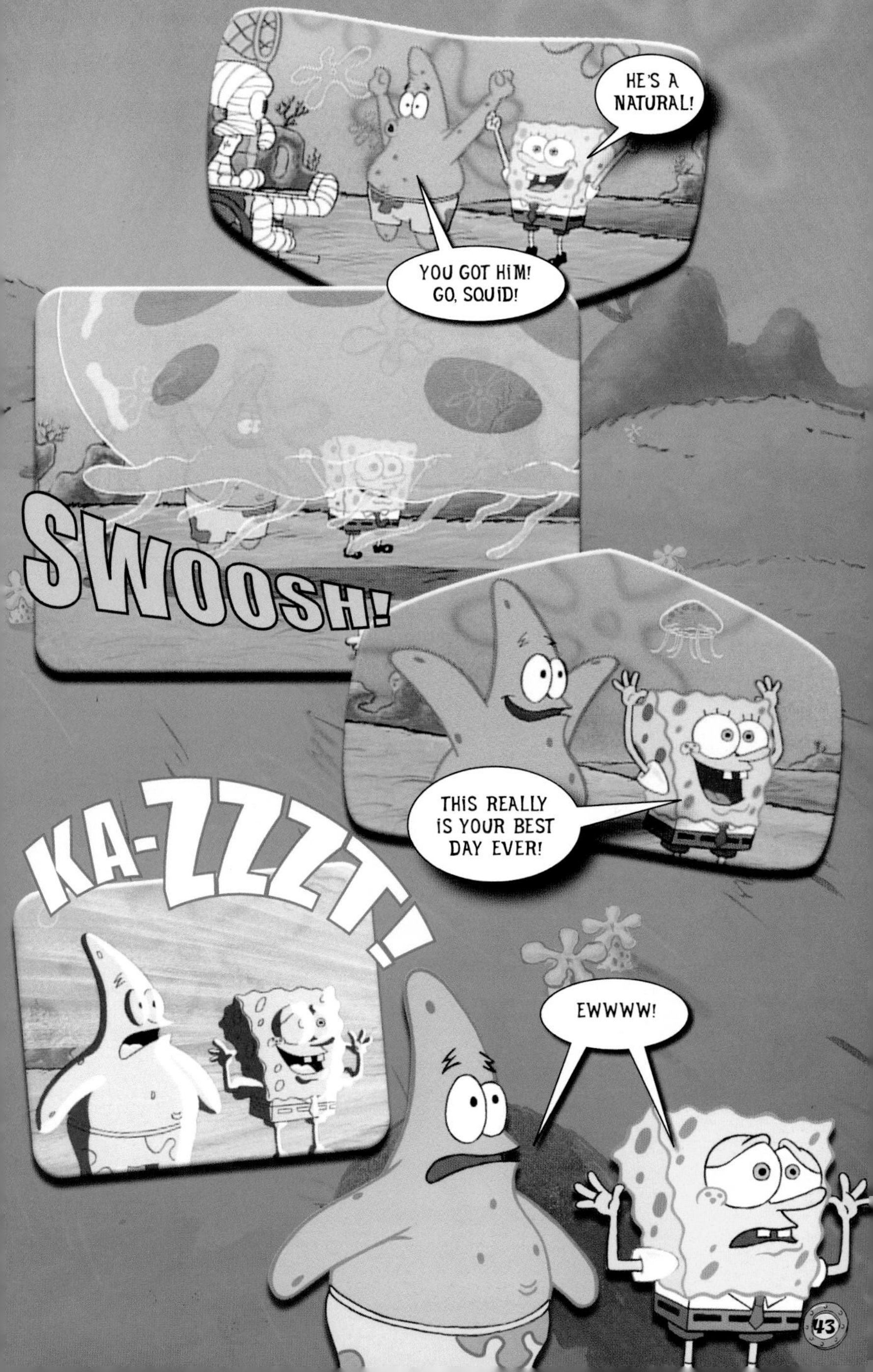
HE'S A NATURAL!
YOU GOT HIM! GO, SQUID!
SWOOSH!
THIS REALLY IS YOUR BEST DAY EVER!
KA-ZZZT!
EWWWW!

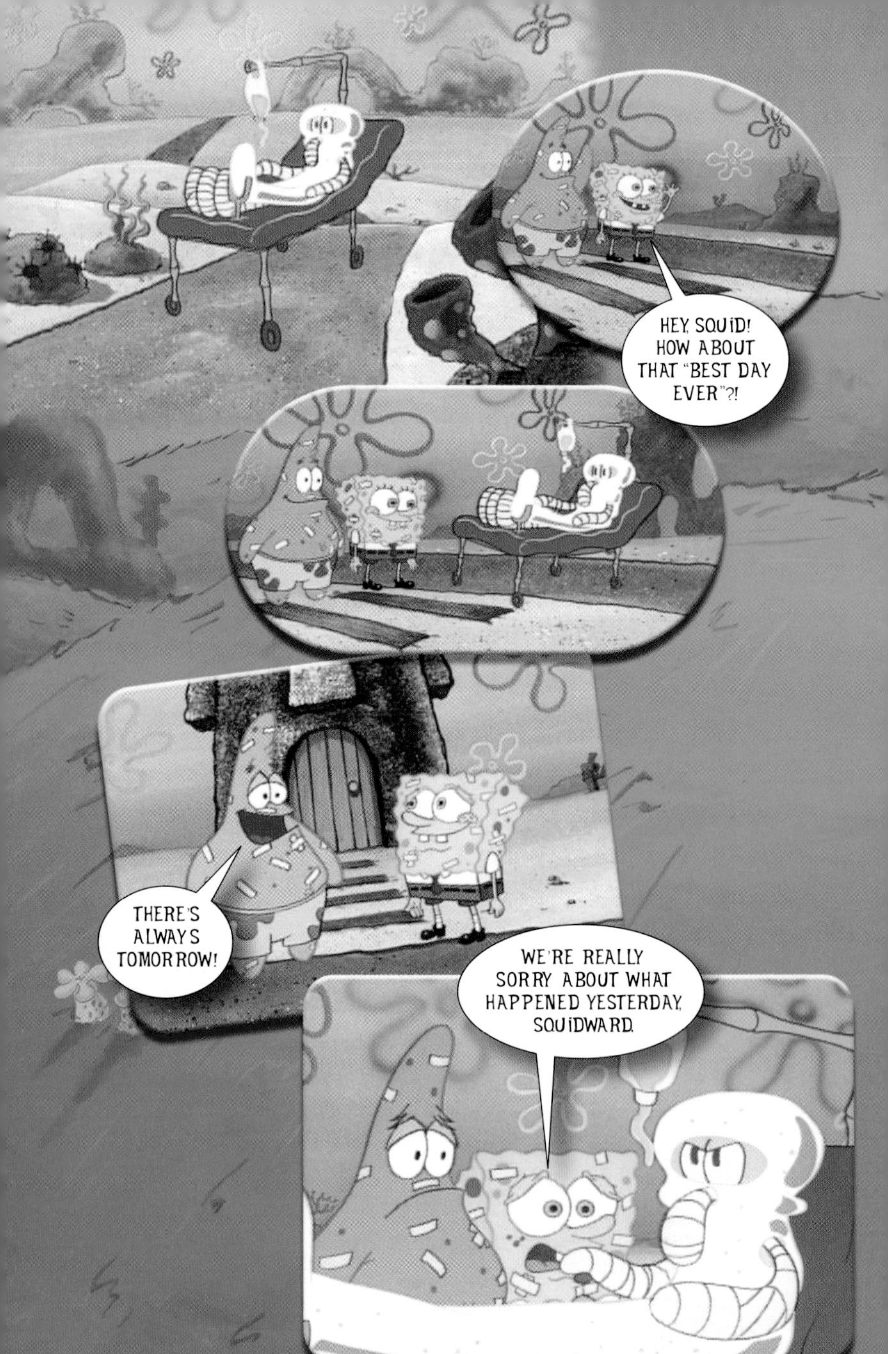
HEY, SQUID! HOW ABOUT THAT "BEST DAY EVER"?!
THERE'S ALWAYS TOMORROW!
WE'RE REALLY SORRY ABOUT WHAT HAPPENED YESTERDAY, SQUIDWARD.

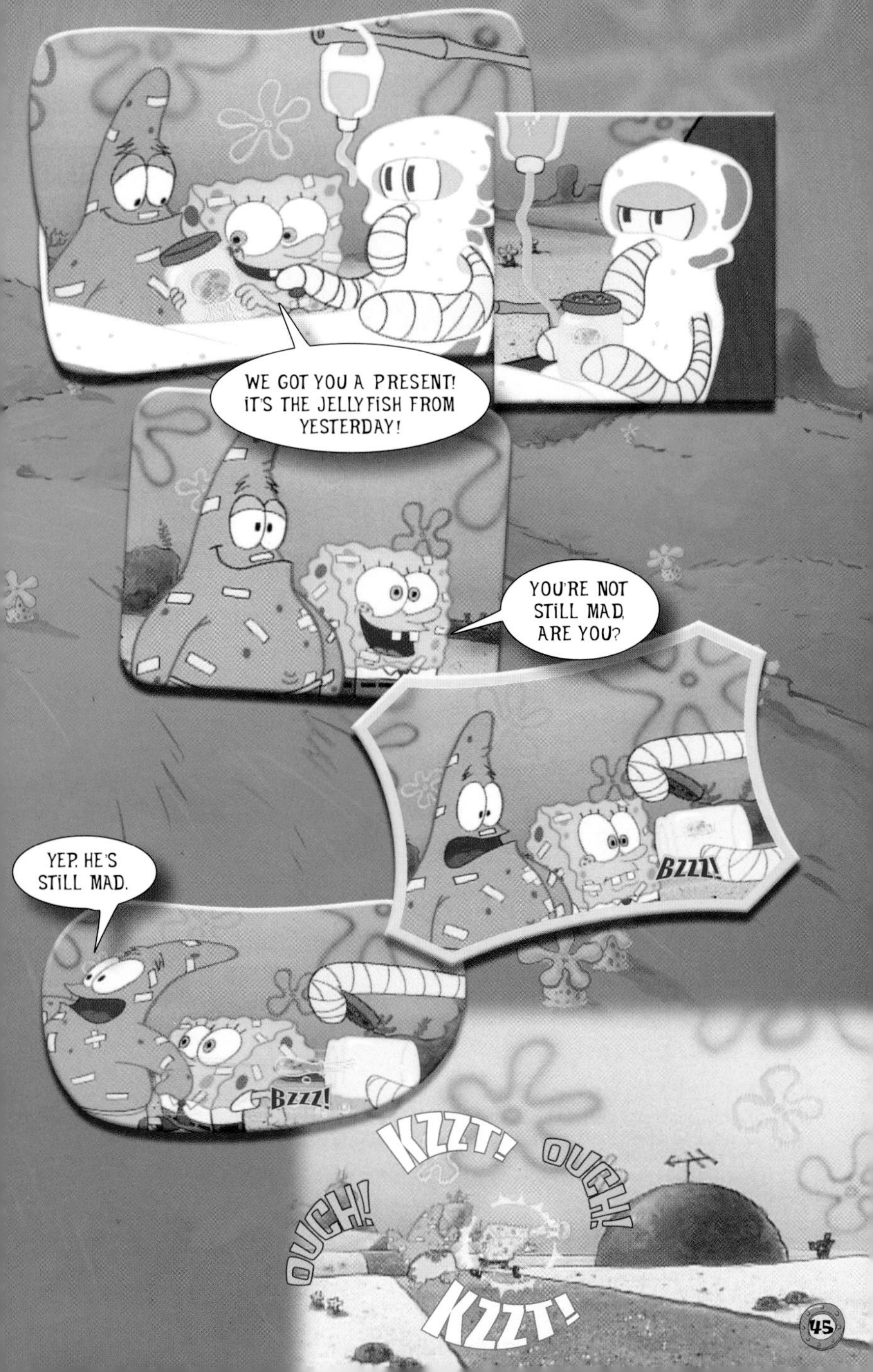
WE GOT YOU A PRESENT! IT'S THE JELLYFISH FROM YESTERDAY!
YOU'RE NOT STILL MAD, ARE YOU?
BZZZ!
YEP, HE'S STILL MAD.
BZZZ!
KZZZT!
OUCH!
OUCH!
KZZZT!

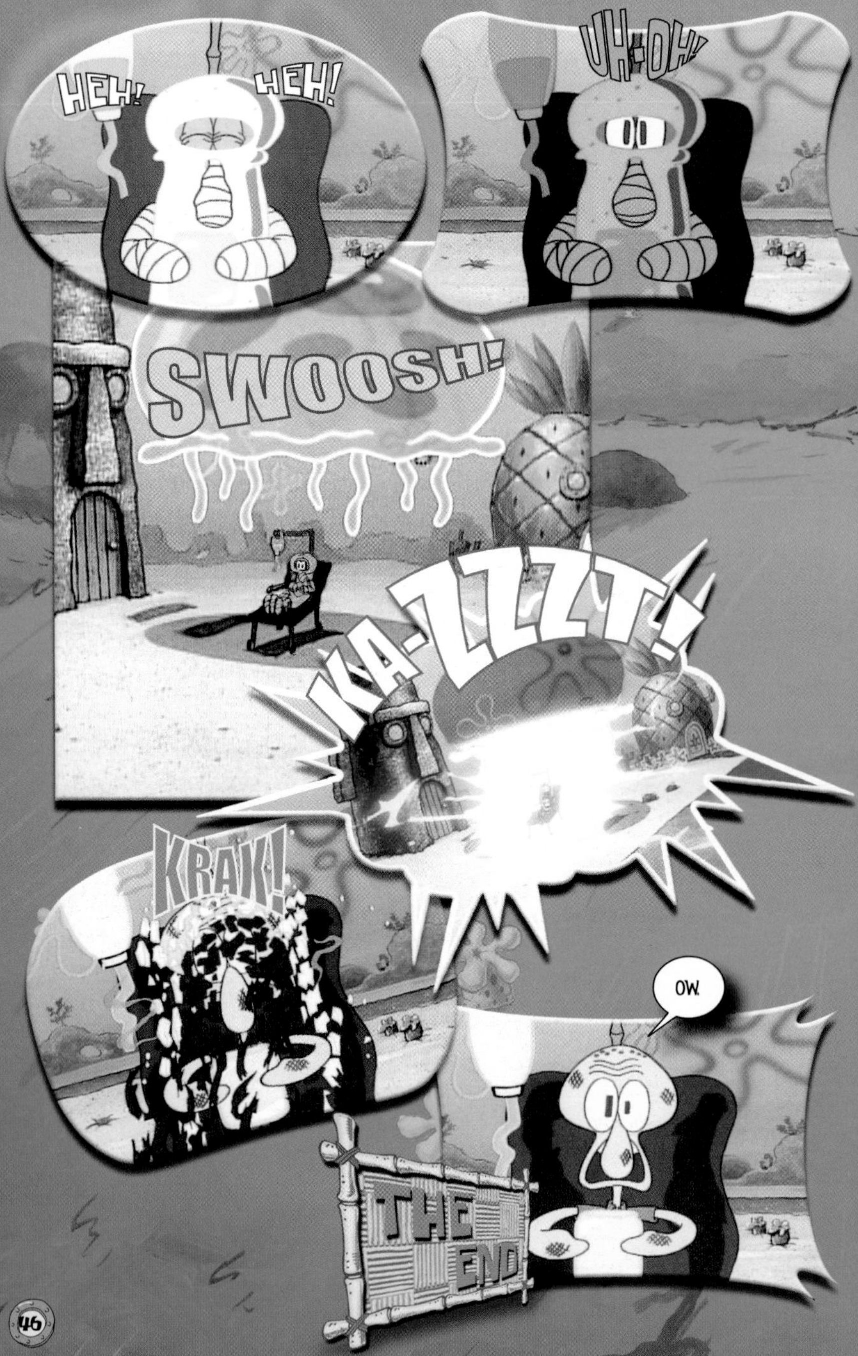
HEH!
HEH!
UH-OH!
SWOOSH!
KA-ZZZZT!
KRAK!
OW.
THE END

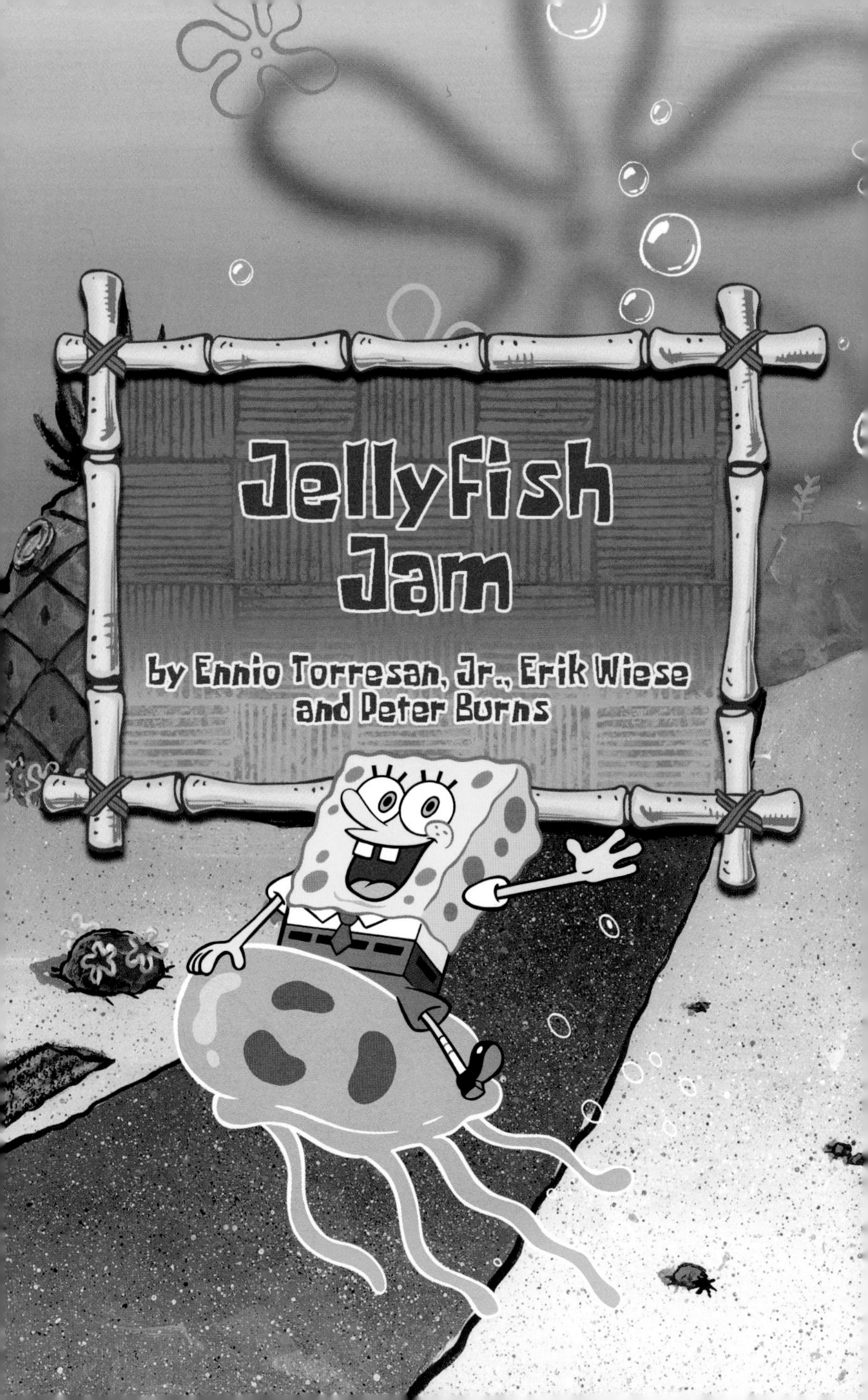
Jellyfish Jam
by Ennio Torresan, Jr., Erik Wiese
and Peter Burns

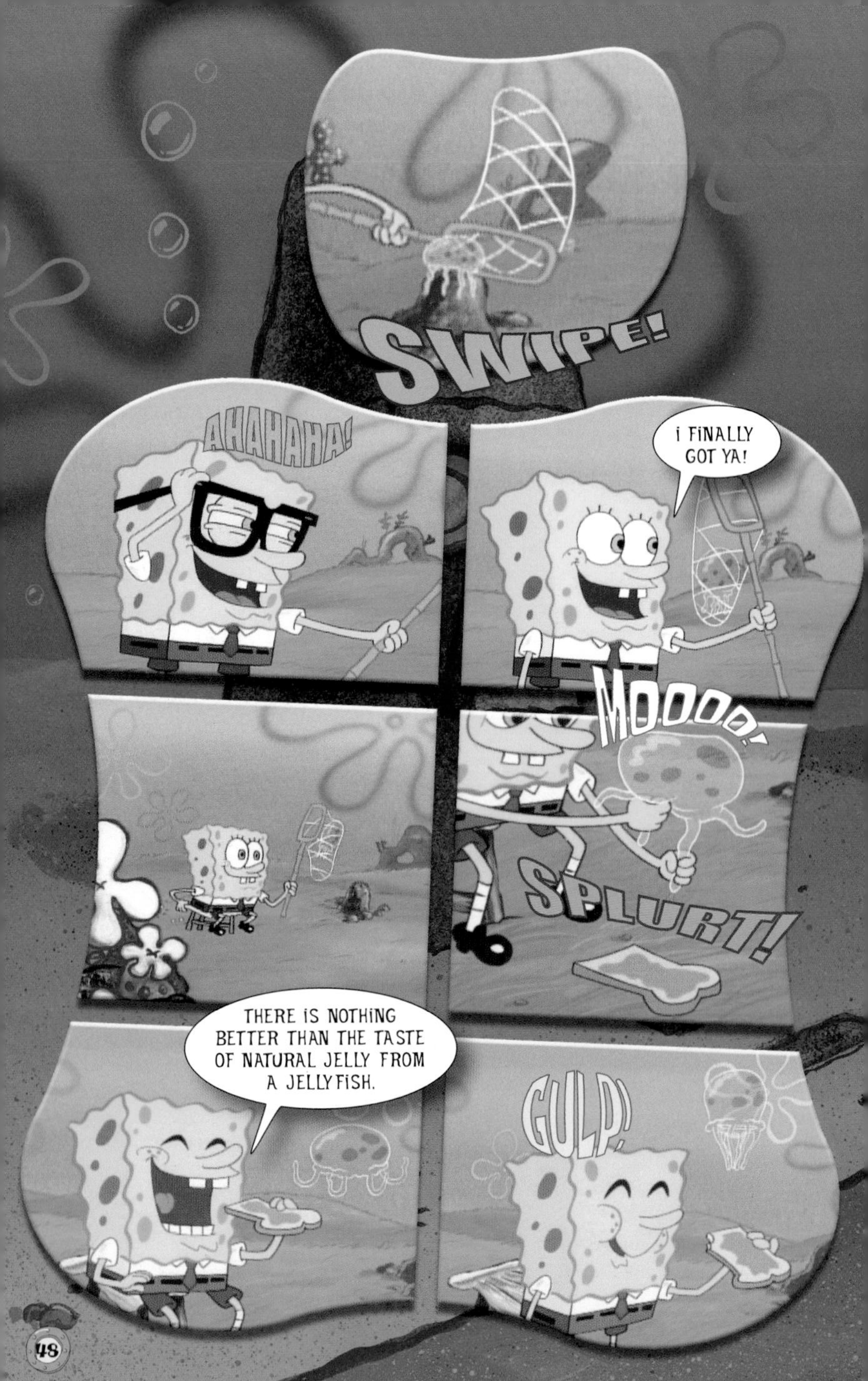
SWIPE!
AHAHAHA!
I FINALLY GOT YA!
MOOOO!
SPLURT!
THERE IS NOTHING BETTER THAN THE TASTE OF NATURAL JELLY FROM A JELLYFISH.
GULP!

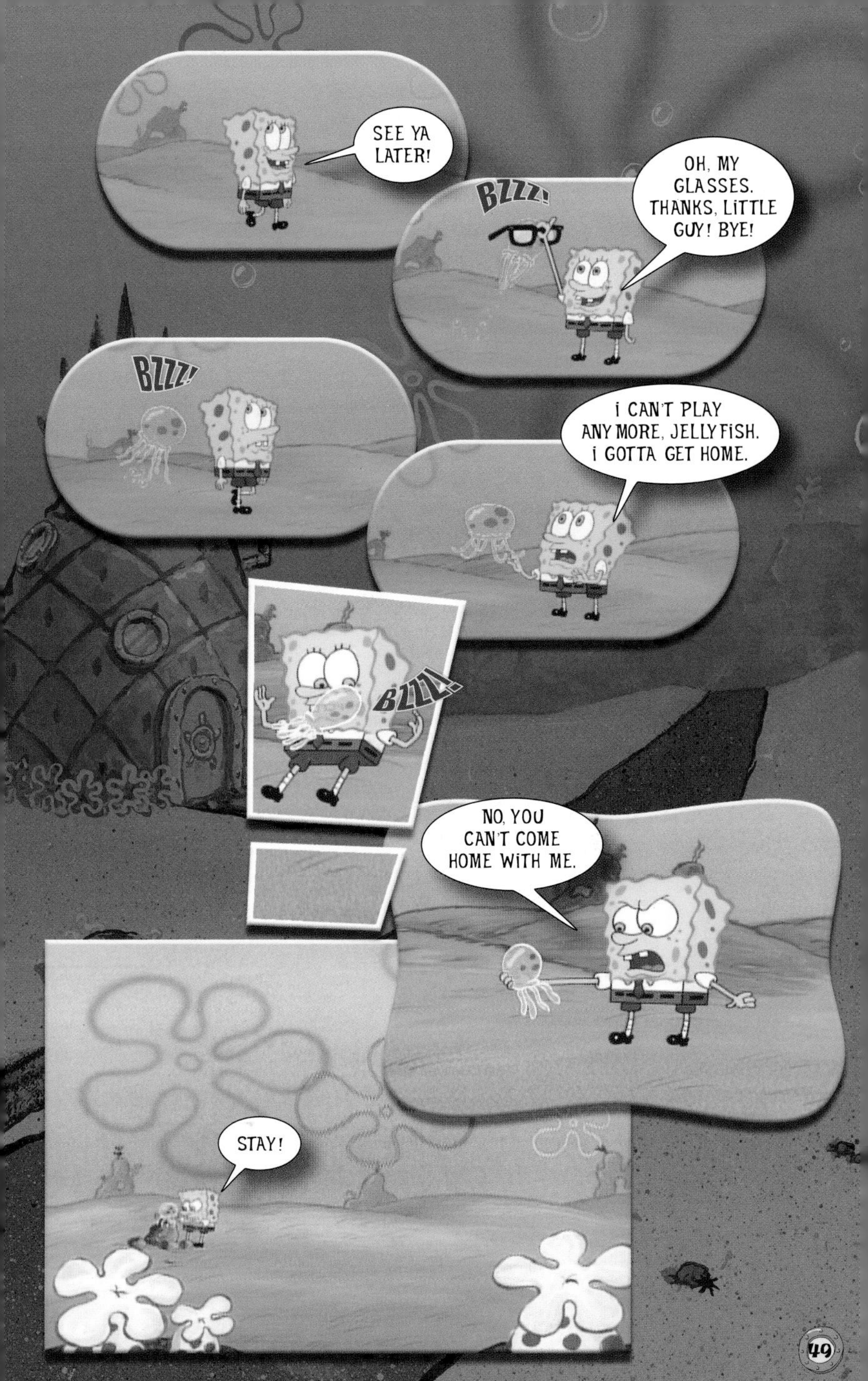
SEE YA LATER!
BZZZ!
OH, MY GLASSES. THANKS, LITTLE GUY! BYE!
BZZZ!
I CAN'T PLAY ANY MORE, JELLYFISH. I GOTTA GET HOME.
BZZZ!
NO, YOU CAN'T COME HOME WITH ME.
STAY!

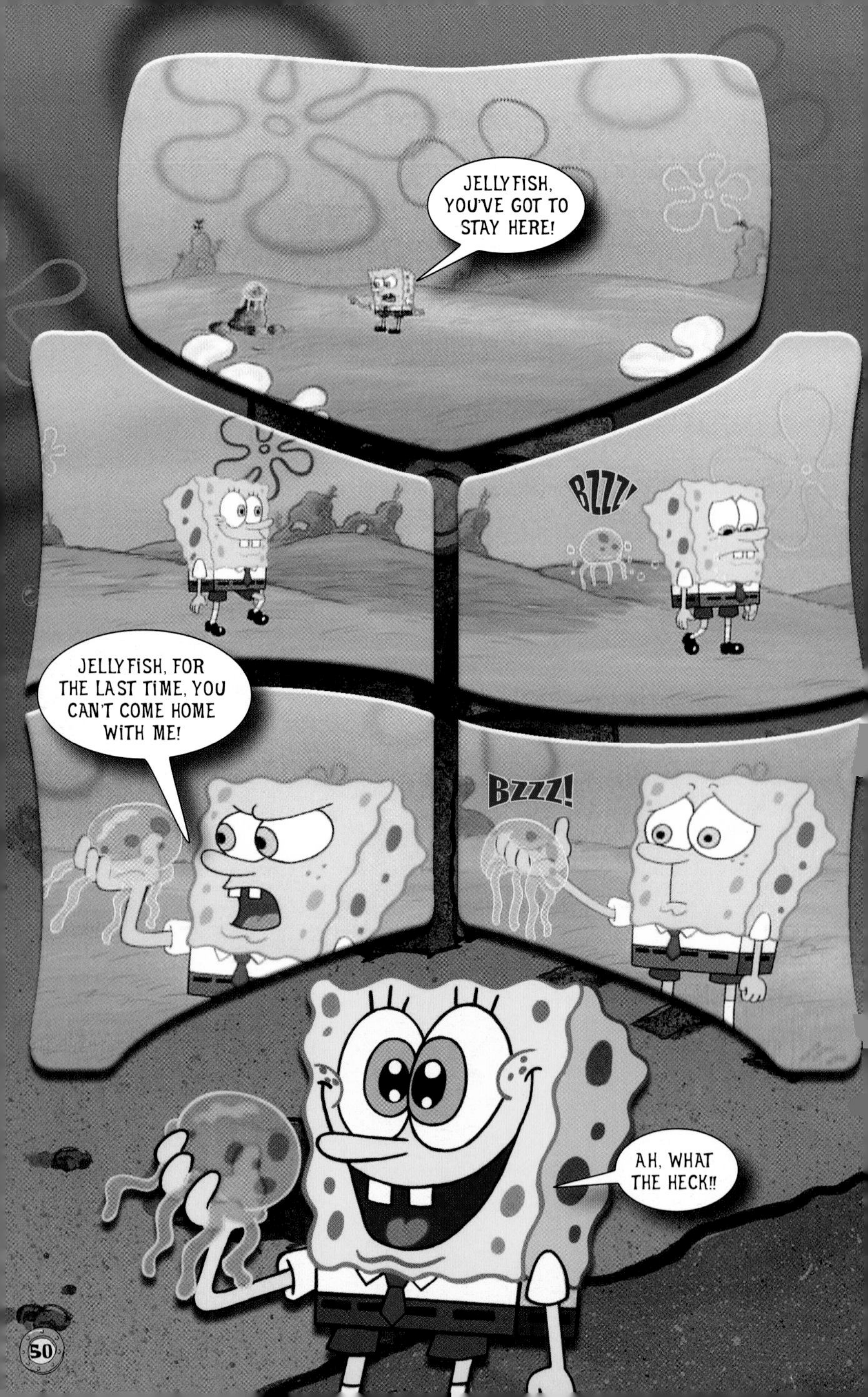
JELLYFISH, YOU'VE GOT TO STAY HERE!
BZZZ!
JELLYFISH, FOR THE LAST TIME, YOU CAN'T COME HOME WITH ME!
BZZZ!
AH, WHAT THE HECK!!

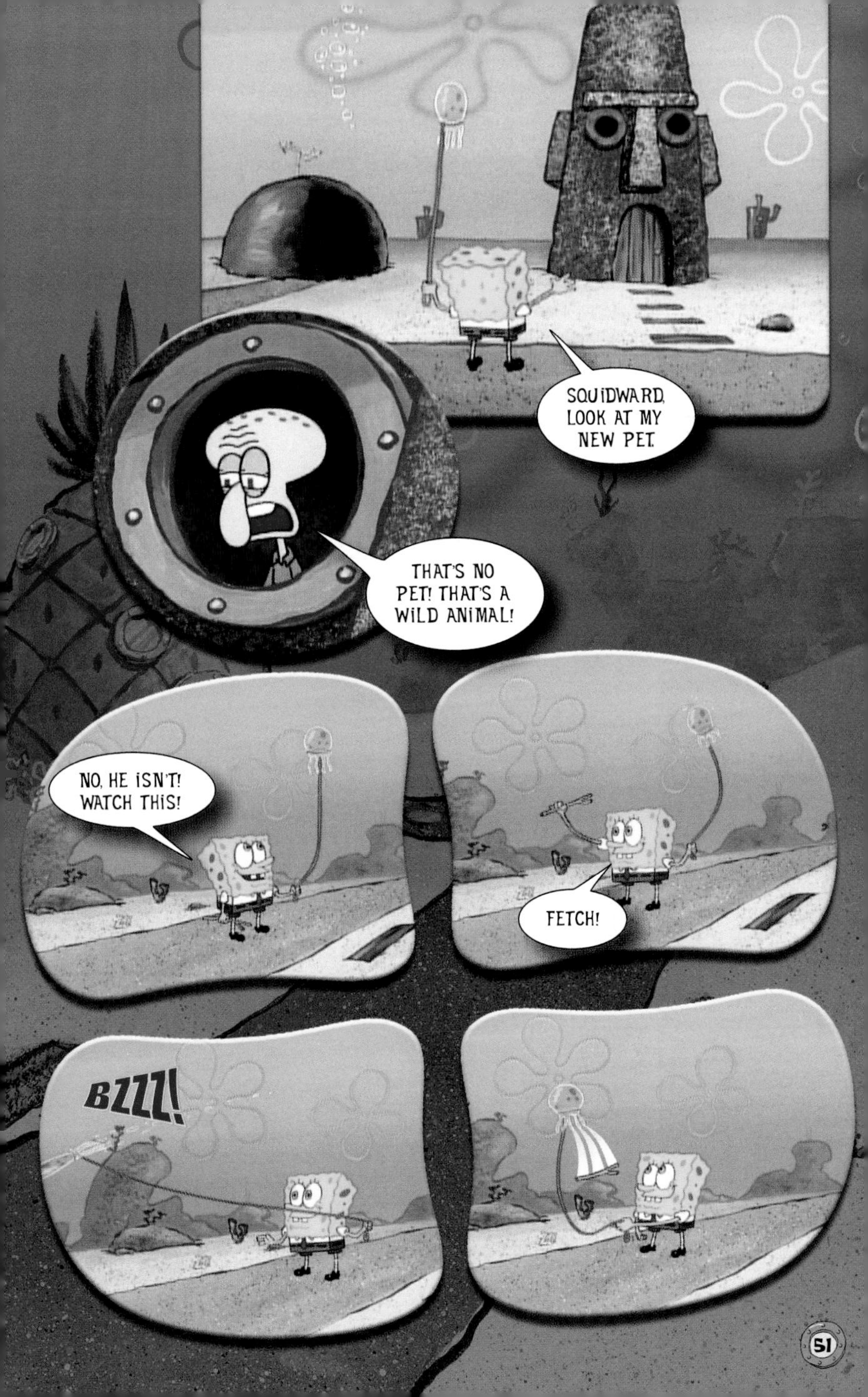
SQUIDWARD, LOOK AT MY NEW PET.
THAT'S NO PET! THAT'S A WILD ANIMAL!
NO, HE ISN'T! WATCH THIS!
FETCH!
BZZZ!

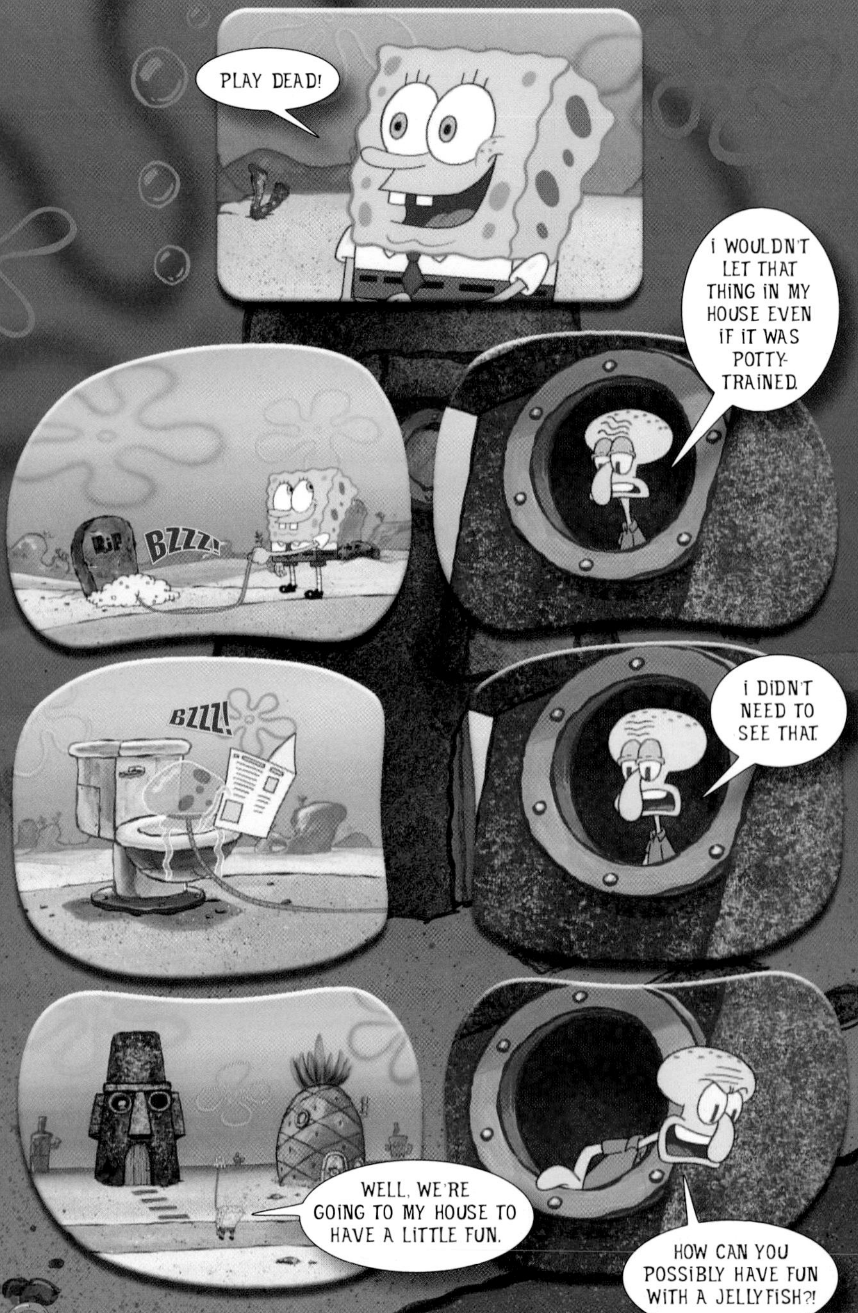
PLAY DEAD!
I WOULDN'T LET THAT THING IN MY HOUSE EVEN IF IT WAS POTTY-TRAINED.
RIP
BZZZ!
BZZZ!
I DIDN'T NEED TO SEE THAT.
WELL, WE'RE GOING TO MY HOUSE TO HAVE A LITTLE FUN.
HOW CAN YOU POSSIBLY HAVE FUN WITH A JELLYFISH?!

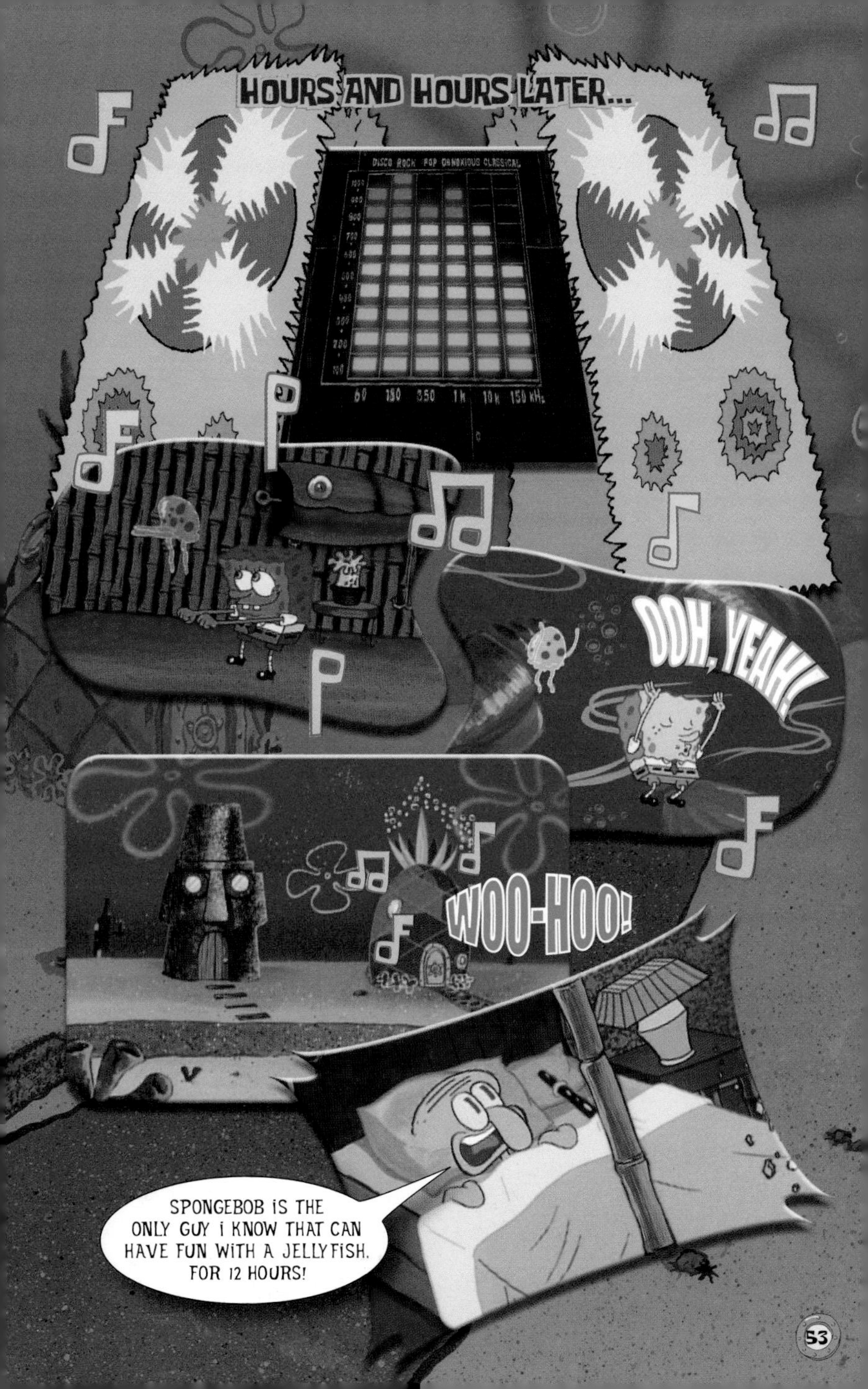
HOURS AND HOURS LATER...
OOH, YEAH!
WOO-HOO!
SPONGEBOB IS THE ONLY GUY I KNOW THAT CAN HAVE FUN WITH A JELLYFISH. FOR 12 HOURS!

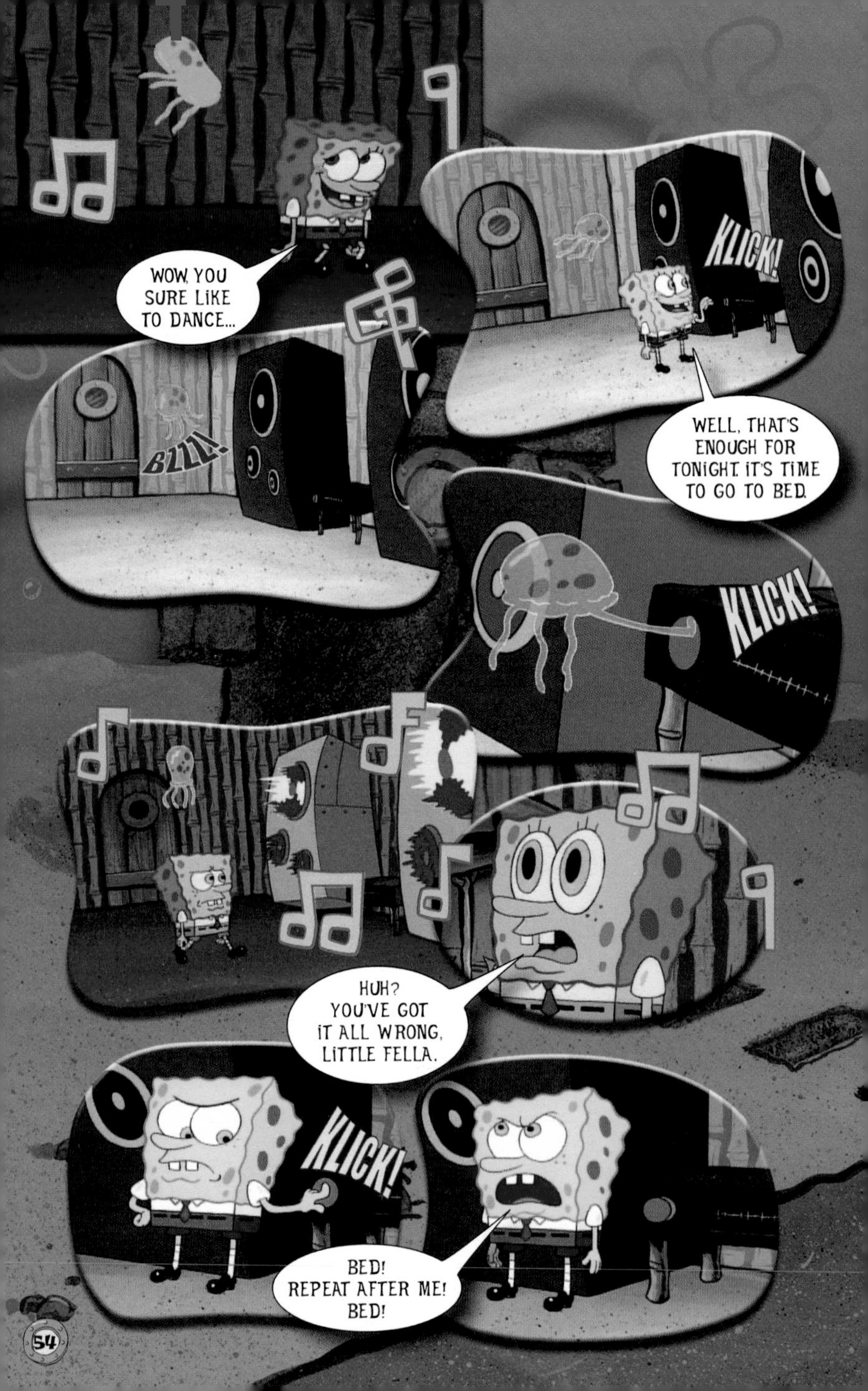
WOW, YOU SURE LIKE TO DANCE...
KLICK!
BZZZ!
WELL, THAT'S ENOUGH FOR TONIGHT. IT'S TIME TO GO TO BED.
KLICK!
HUH? YOU'VE GOT IT ALL WRONG, LITTLE FELLA.
KLICK!
BED! REPEAT AFTER ME! BED!

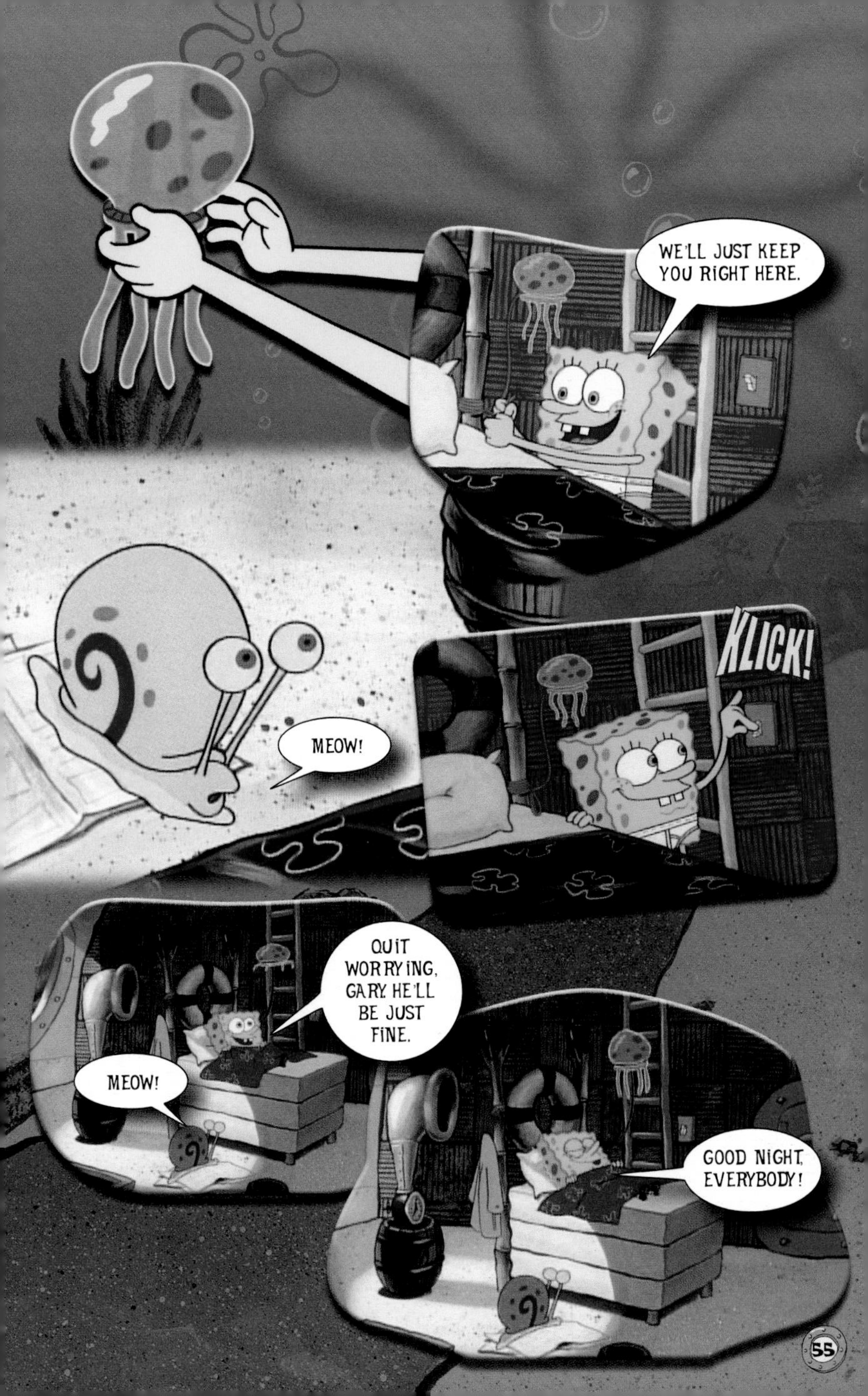
WE'LL JUST KEEP YOU RIGHT HERE.
MEOW!
KLICK!
QUIT WORRYING, GARY. HE'LL BE JUST FINE.
MEOW!
GOOD NIGHT, EVERYBODY!

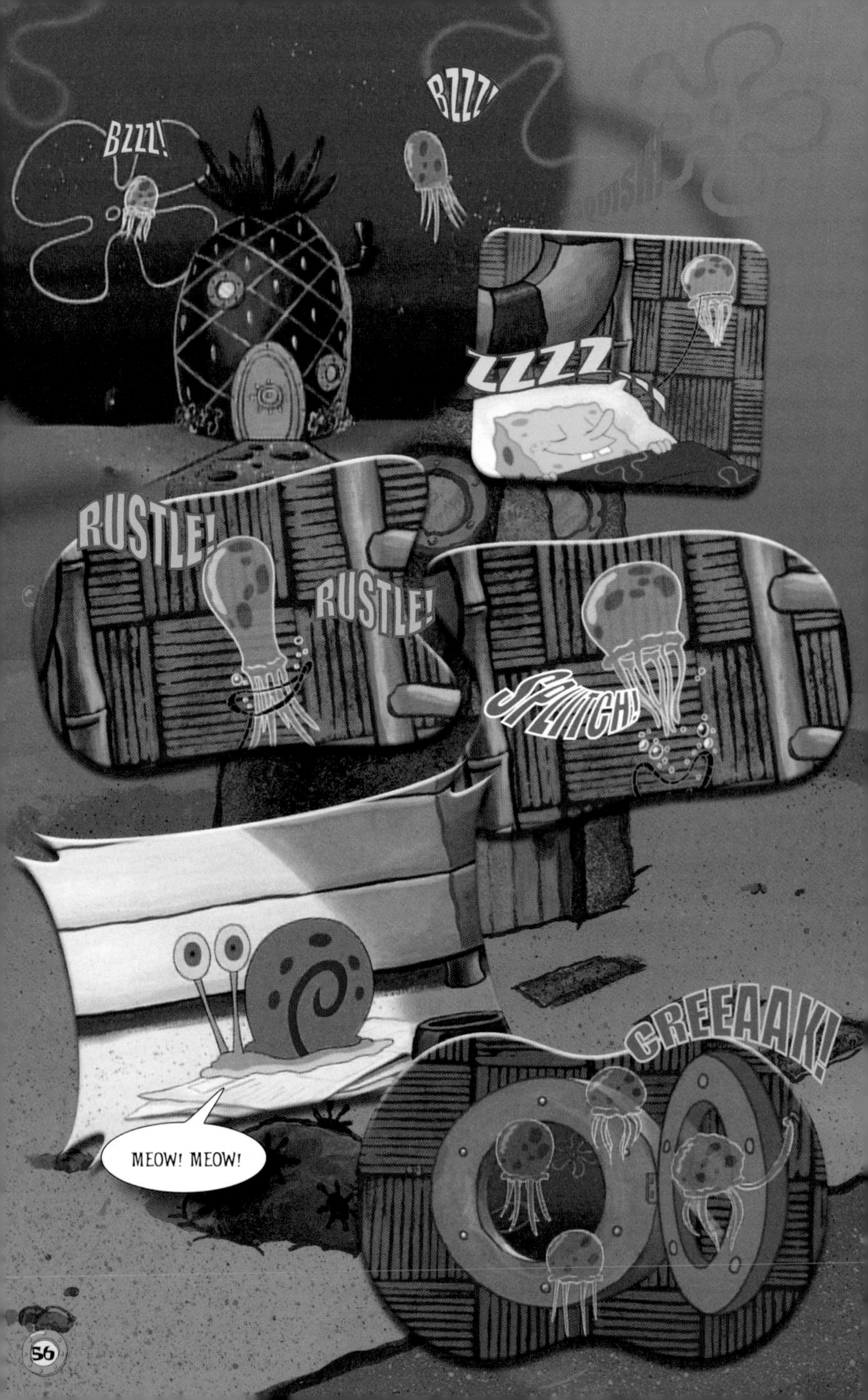
BZZZ!
BZZZ!
ZZZZ
RUSTLE!
RUSTLE!
MEOW! MEOW!
CREEAAK!

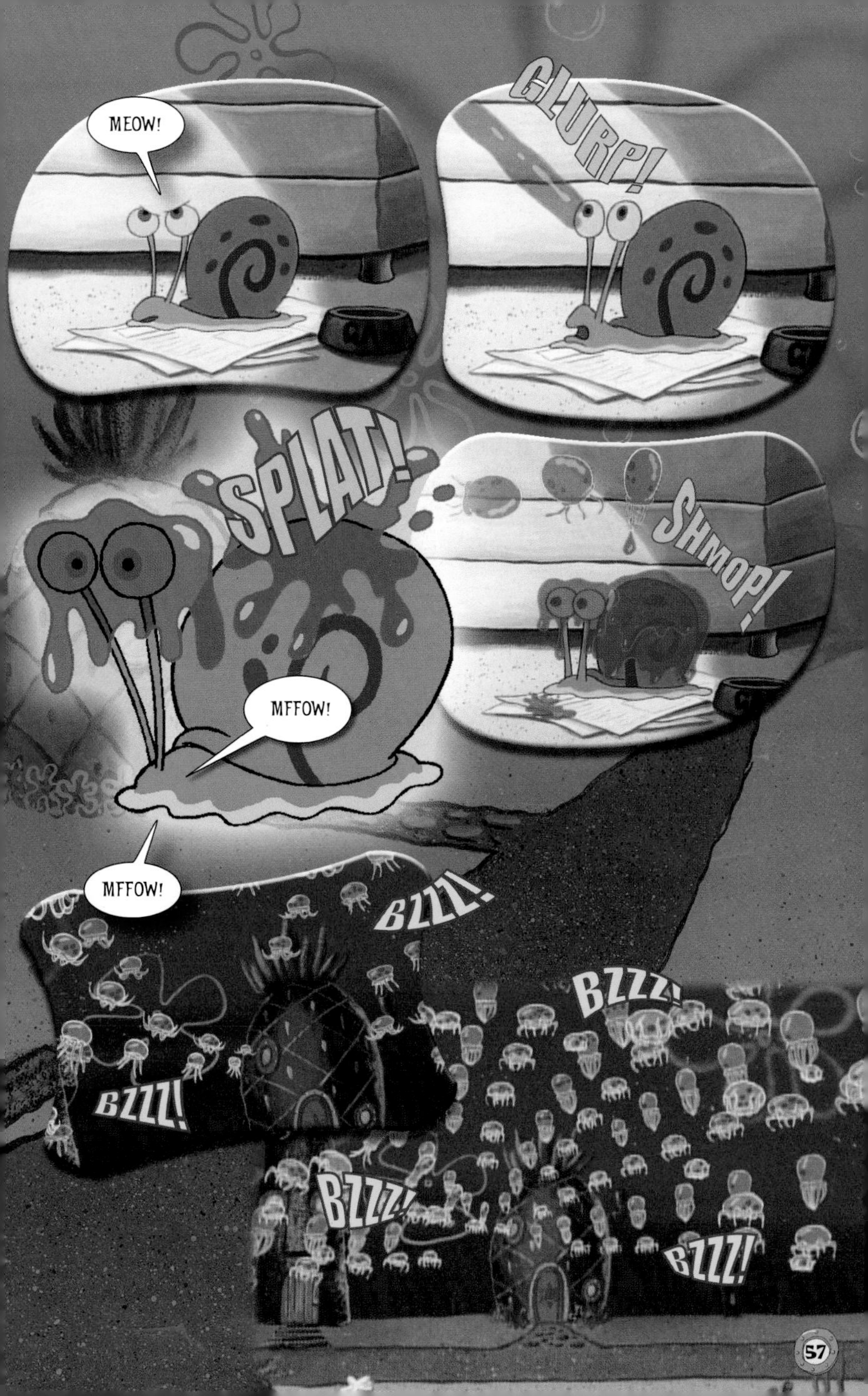
MEOW!
GLURP!
SPLAT!
SHMOP!
MFFOW!
MFFOW!
BZZZ!
BZZZ!
BZZZ!
BZZZ!
BZZZ!

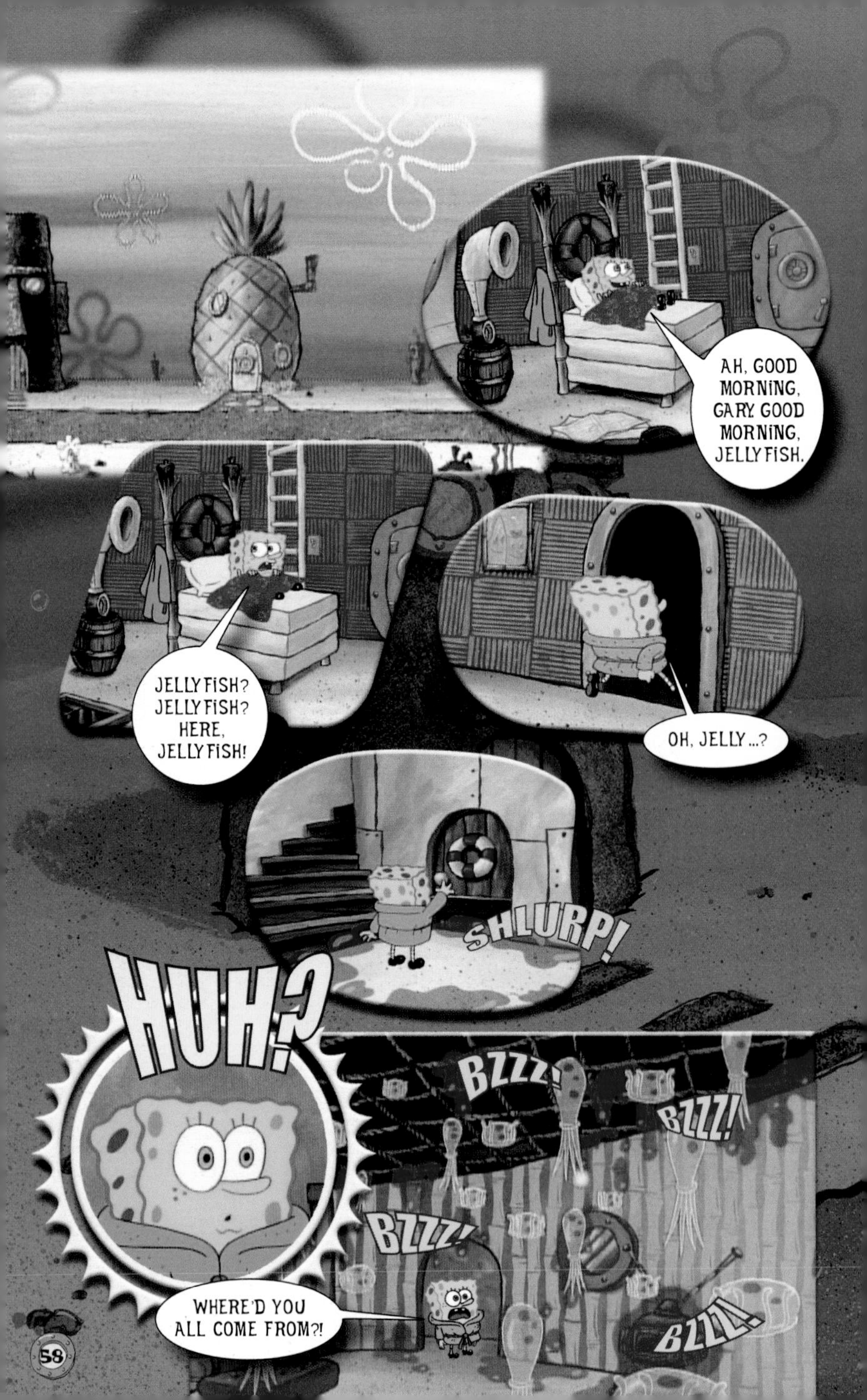
AH, GOOD MORNING, GARY. GOOD MORNING, JELLYFISH.
JELLYFISH? JELLYFISH? HERE, JELLYFISH!
OH, JELLY...?
SHLURP!
HUH?
BZZZ!
BZZZ!
BZZZ!
BZZZ!
WHERE'D YOU ALL COME FROM?!

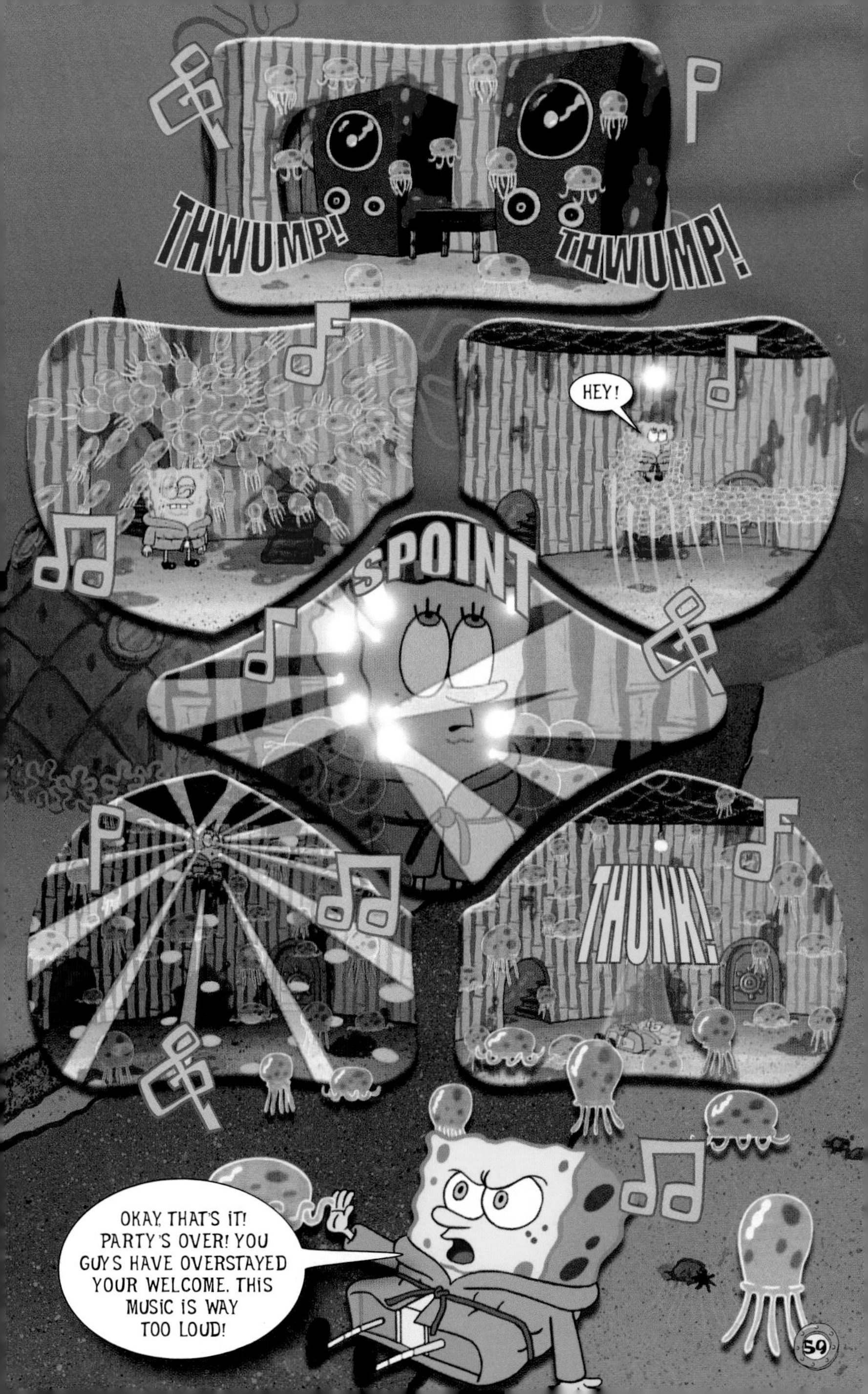
THWUMP!
THWUMP!
HEY!
SPOINT
THUNK!
OKAY, THAT'S IT! PARTY'S OVER! YOU GUYS HAVE OVERSTAYED YOUR WELCOME. THIS MUSIC IS WAY TOO LOUD!

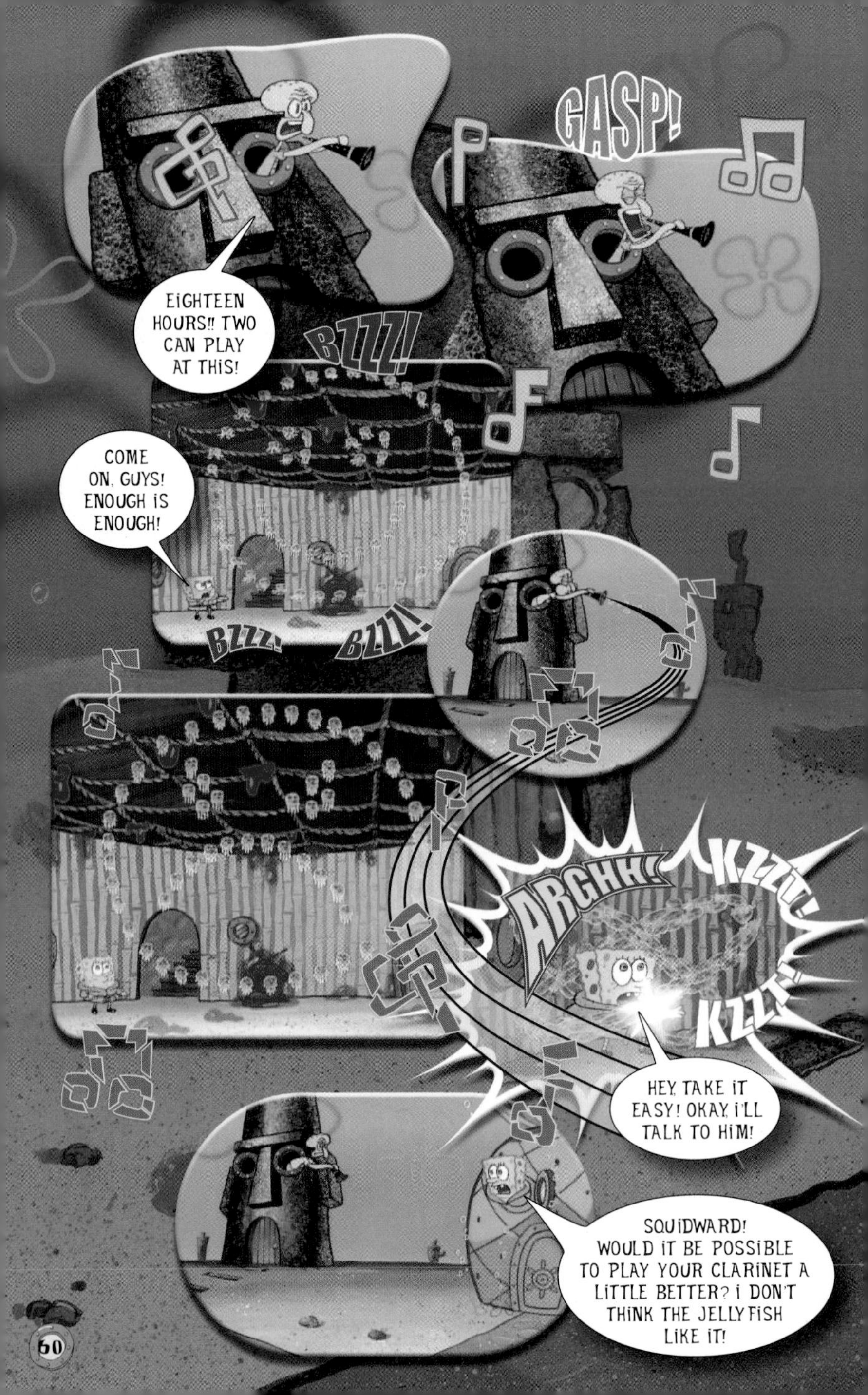
GASP!
EIGHTEEN HOURS!! TWO CAN PLAY AT THIS!
BZZZ!
COME ON, GUYS! ENOUGH IS ENOUGH!
BZZZ!
BZZZ!
ARGHH!
KZZT!
KZZT!
HEY, TAKE IT EASY! OKAY, I'LL TALK TO HIM!
SQUIDWARD! WOULD IT BE POSSIBLE TO PLAY YOUR CLARINET A LITTLE BETTER? I DON'T THINK THE JELLYFISH LIKE IT!

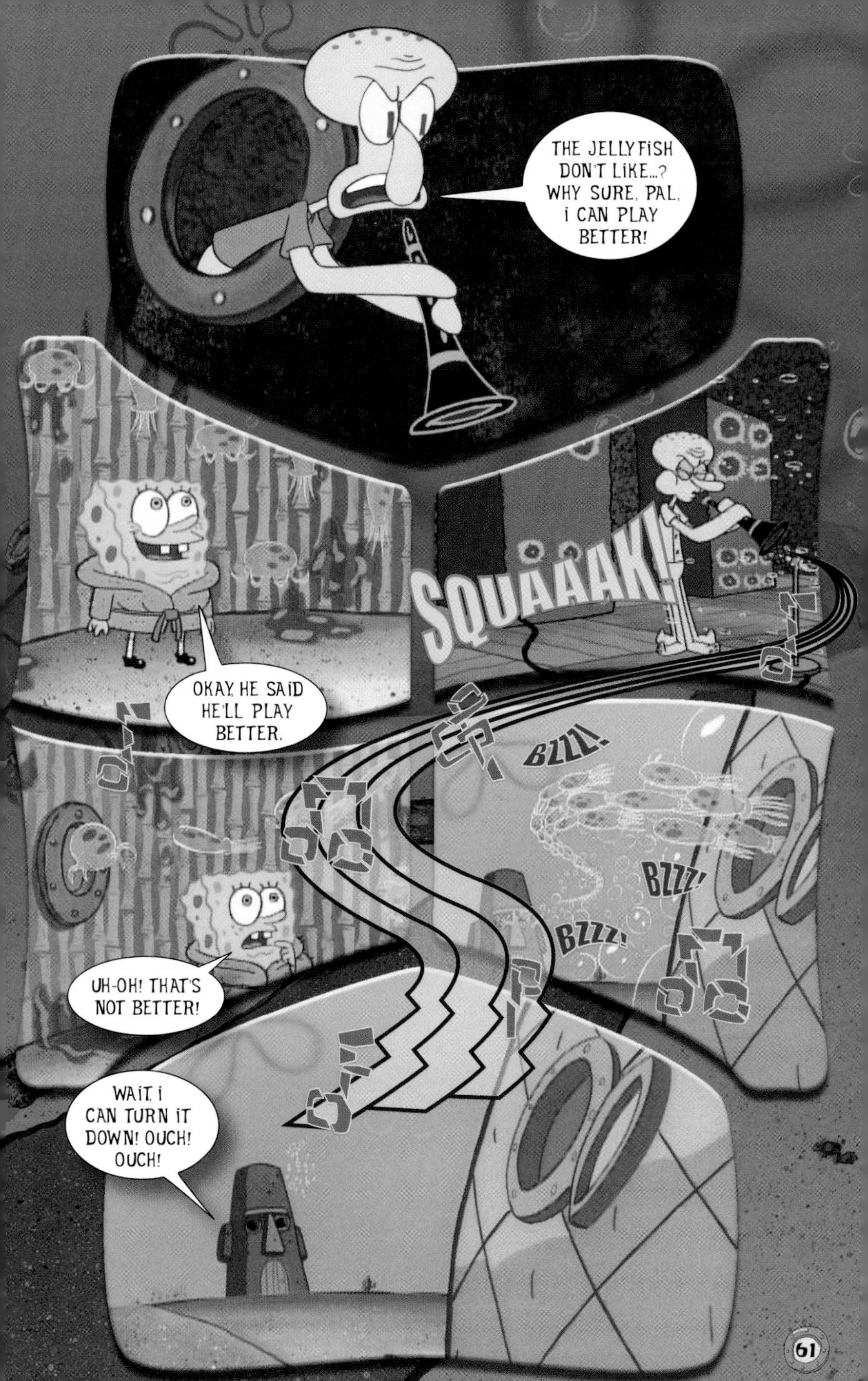
THE JELLYFISH DON'T LIKE...? WHY SURE, PAL, I CAN PLAY BETTER!
OKAY, HE SAID HE'LL PLAY BETTER.
SQUAAAK!
BZZZ!
BZZZ!
BZZZ!
UH-OH! THAT'S NOT BETTER!
WAIT, I CAN TURN IT DOWN! OUCH! OUCH!

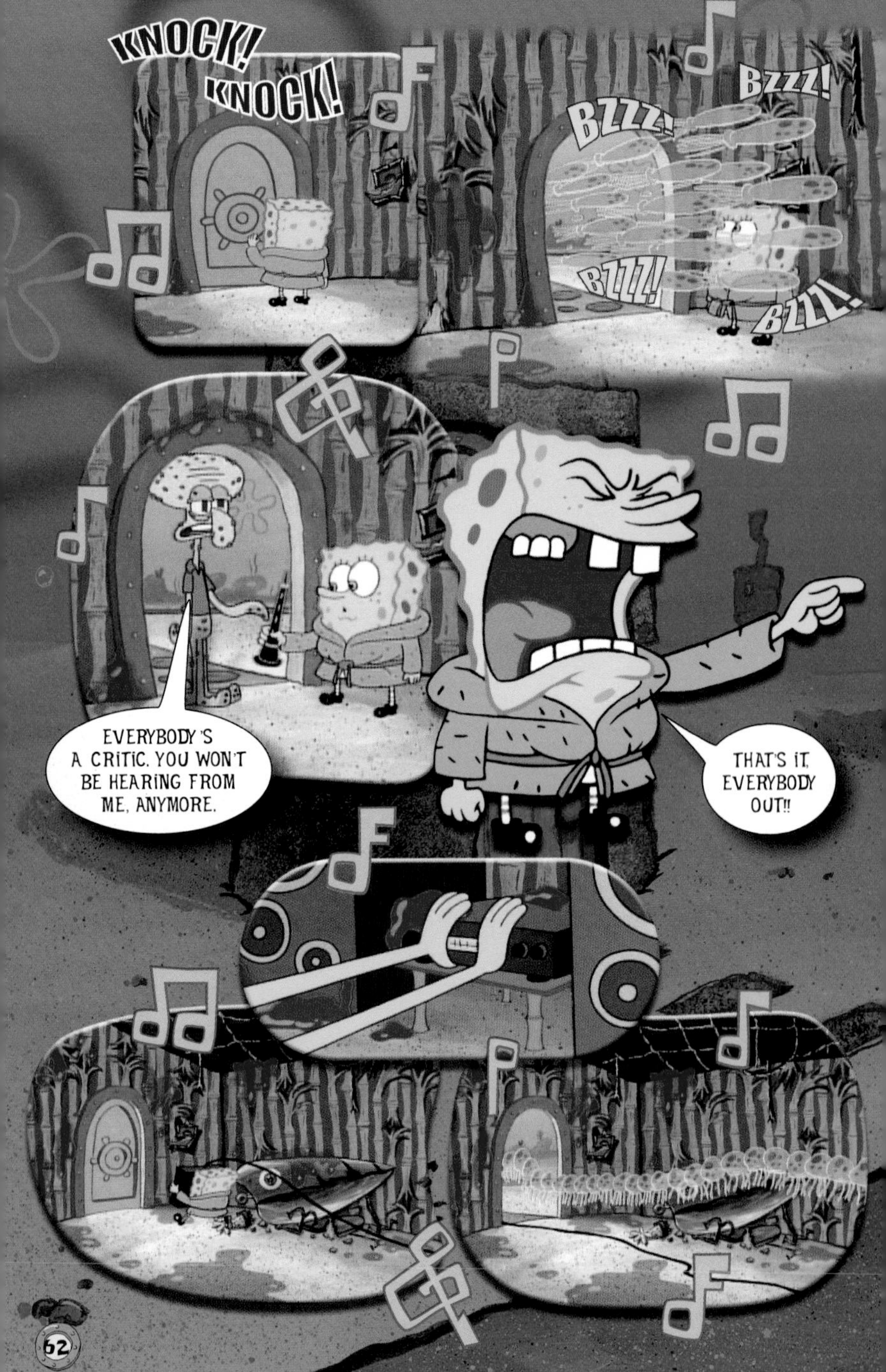
KNOCK! KNOCK!
BZZZ! BZZZ! BZZZ! BZZZ!
EVERYBODY'S A CRITIC. YOU WON'T BE HEARING FROM ME, ANYMORE.
THAT'S IT, EVERYBODY OUT!!

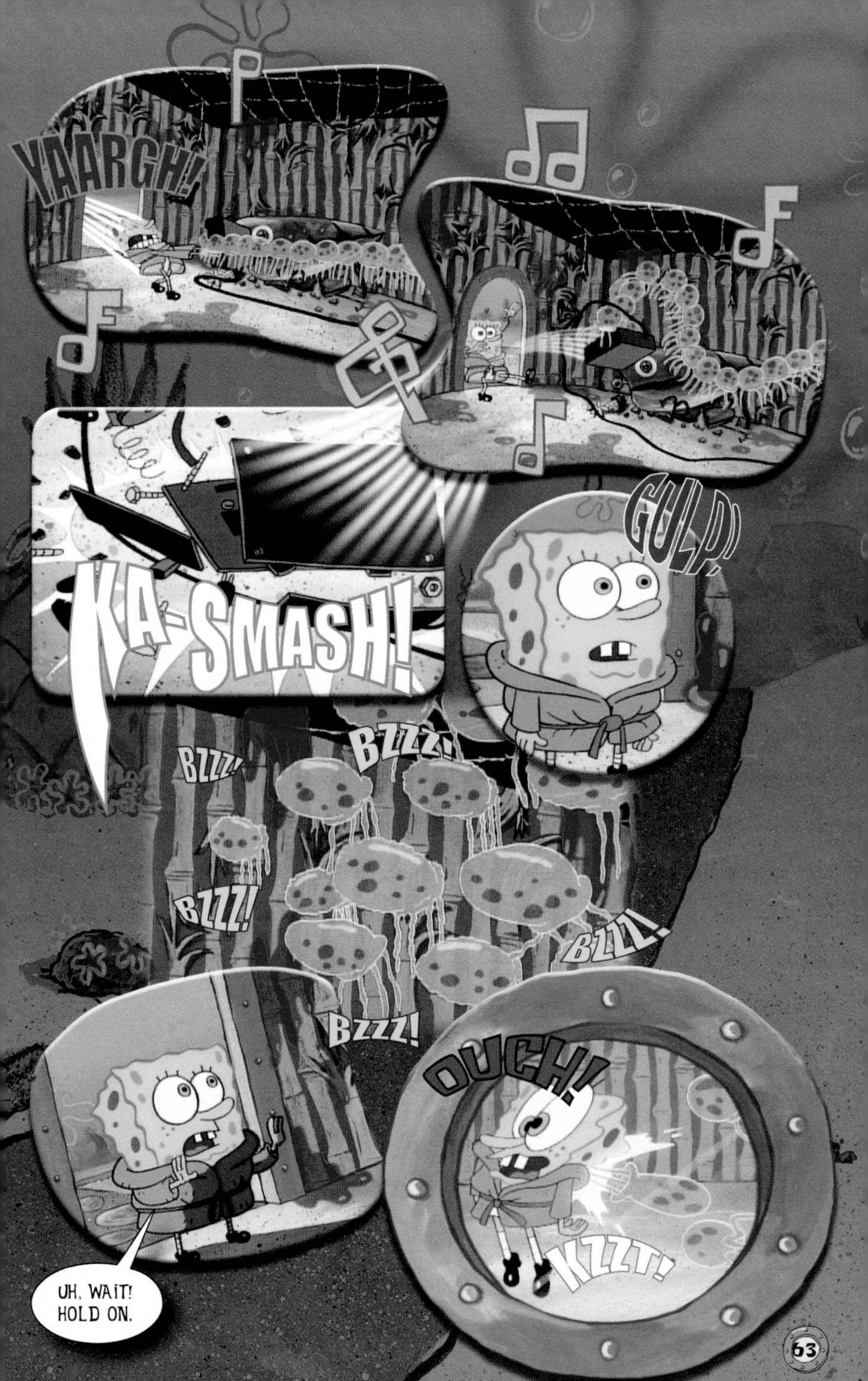
YAARGH!
KA-SMASH!
GULP!
BZZZ!
BZZZ!
BZZZ!
BZZZ!
BZZZ!
UH, WAIT! HOLD ON.
OUCH!
KZZZT!

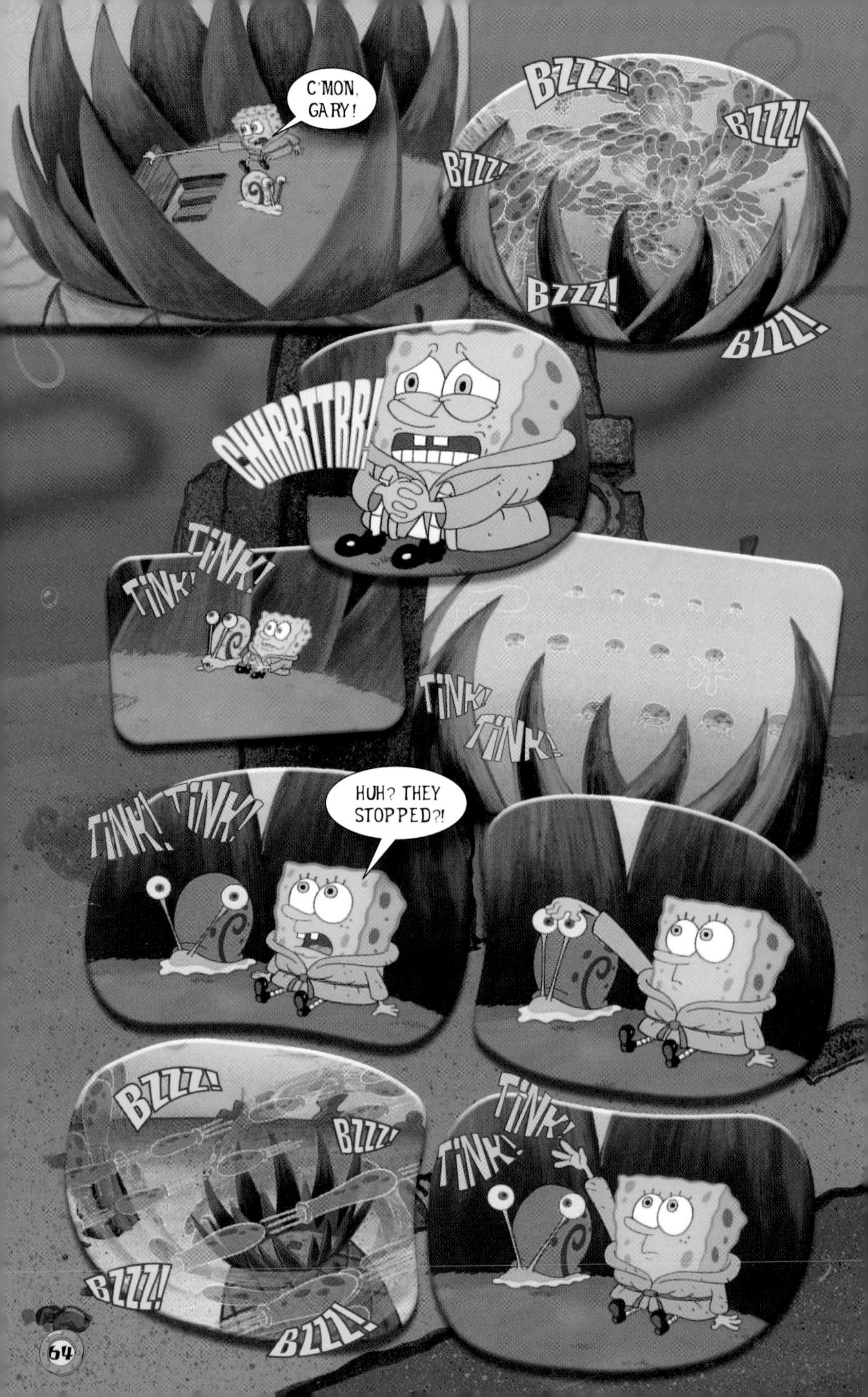
C'MON, GARY!
BZZZ!
BZZZ!
BZZZ!
BZZZ!
BZZZ!
CHRRTTRR!
TINK! TINK!
TINK! TINK!
TINK! TINK!
HUH? THEY STOPPED?!
BZZZ!
BZZZ!
BZZZ!
BZZZ!
TINK! TINK!

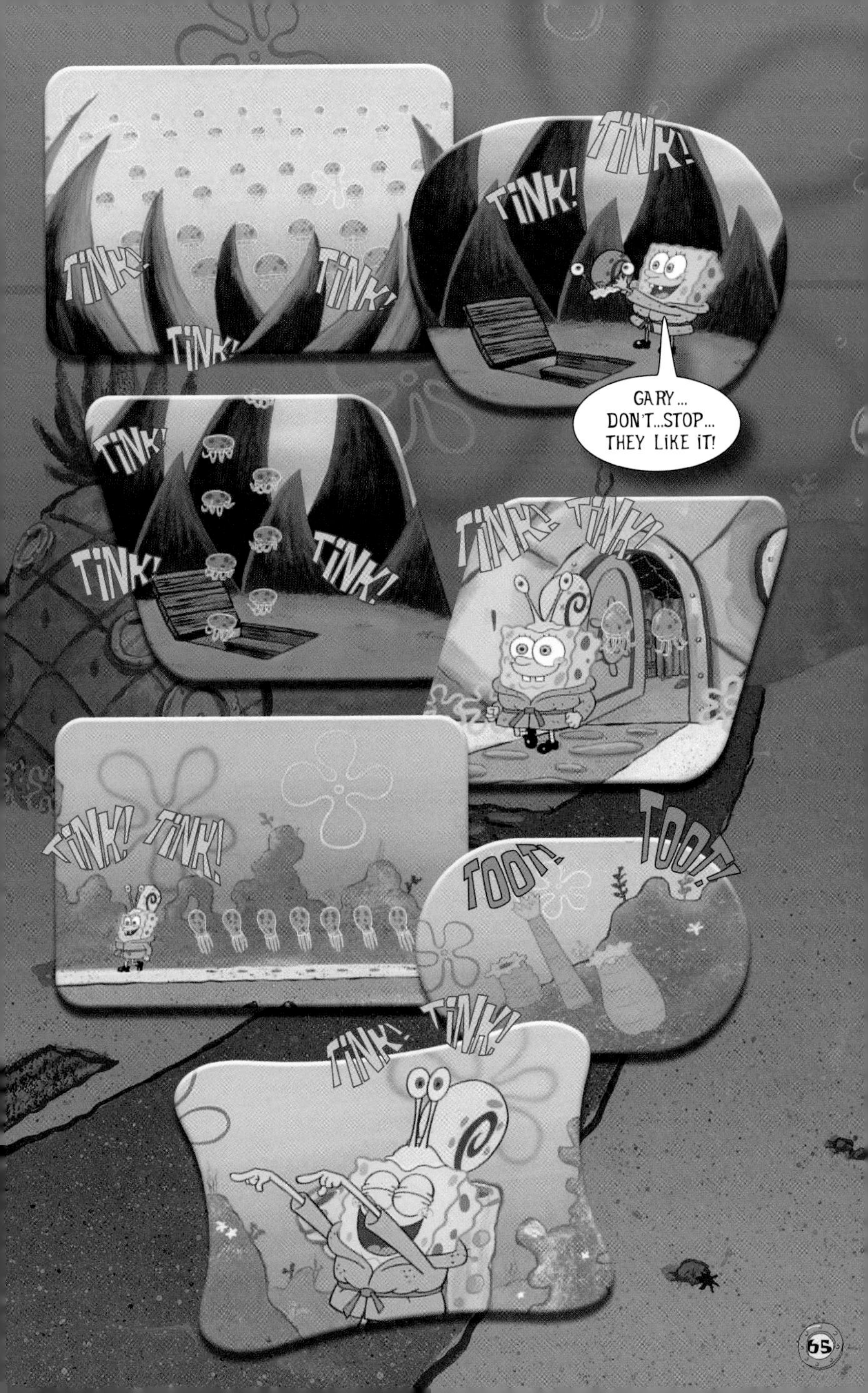
TINK!
TINK!
TINK!
TINK!
TINK!
GARY... DON'T...STOP... THEY LIKE IT!
TINK!
TINK!
TINK!
TINK!
TINK!
TINK!
TINK!
TOOT!
TOOT!
TINK!
TINK!

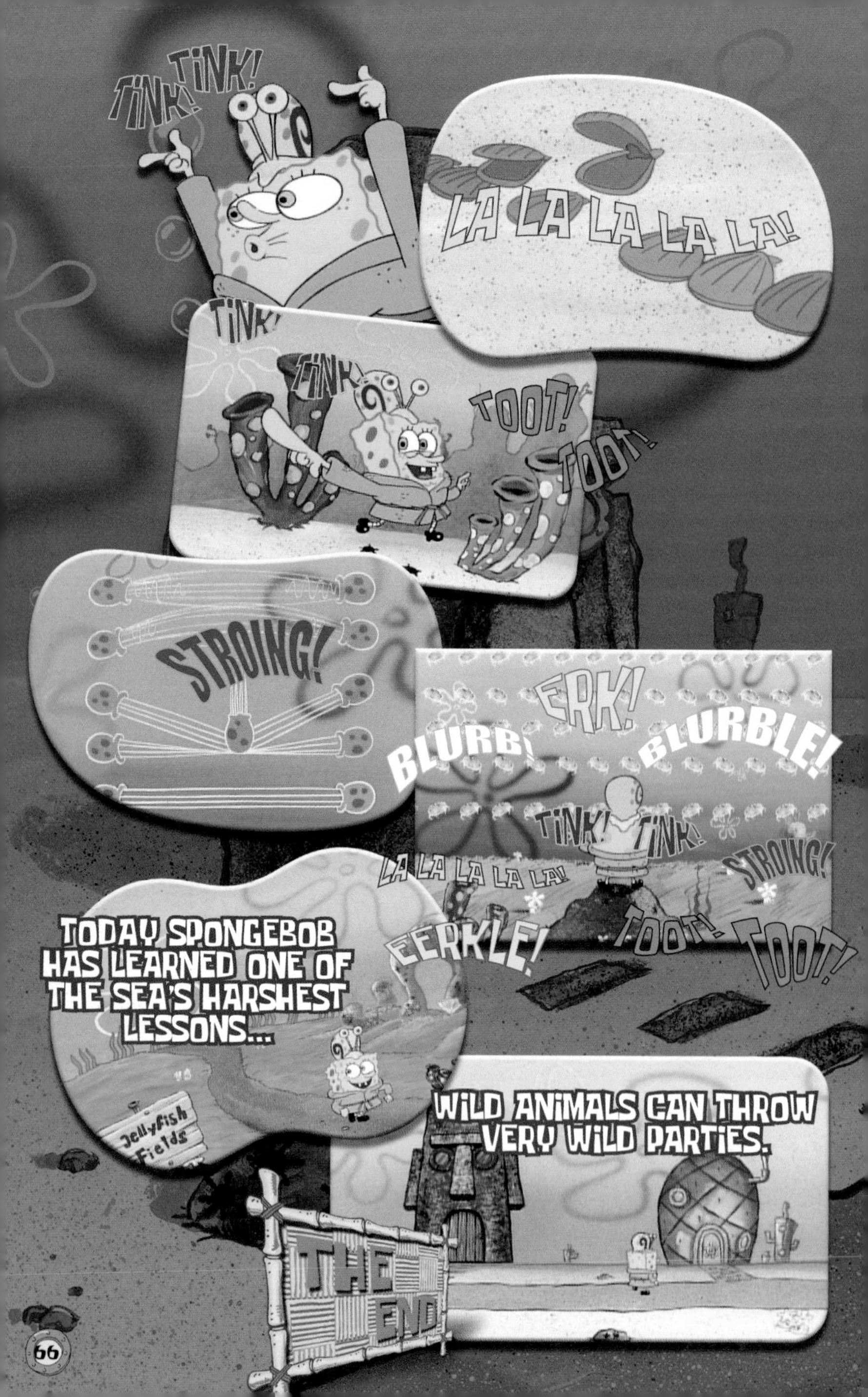
TINK! TINK!
LA LA LA LA LA!
TINK!
TINK!
TOOT!
TOOT!
STROING!
ERK!
BLURB!
BLURBLE!
TINK! TINK!
LA LA LA LA LA!
STROING!
EERKLE!
TOOT!
TOOT!
TODAY SPONGEBOB HAS LEARNED ONE OF THE SEA'S HARSHEST LESSONS...
Jellyfish Fields
WILD ANIMALS CAN THROW VERY WILD PARTIES.
THE END

JellyFish Hunter

by Walt Dohrn, Paul Tibbitt
and Mark O'Hare

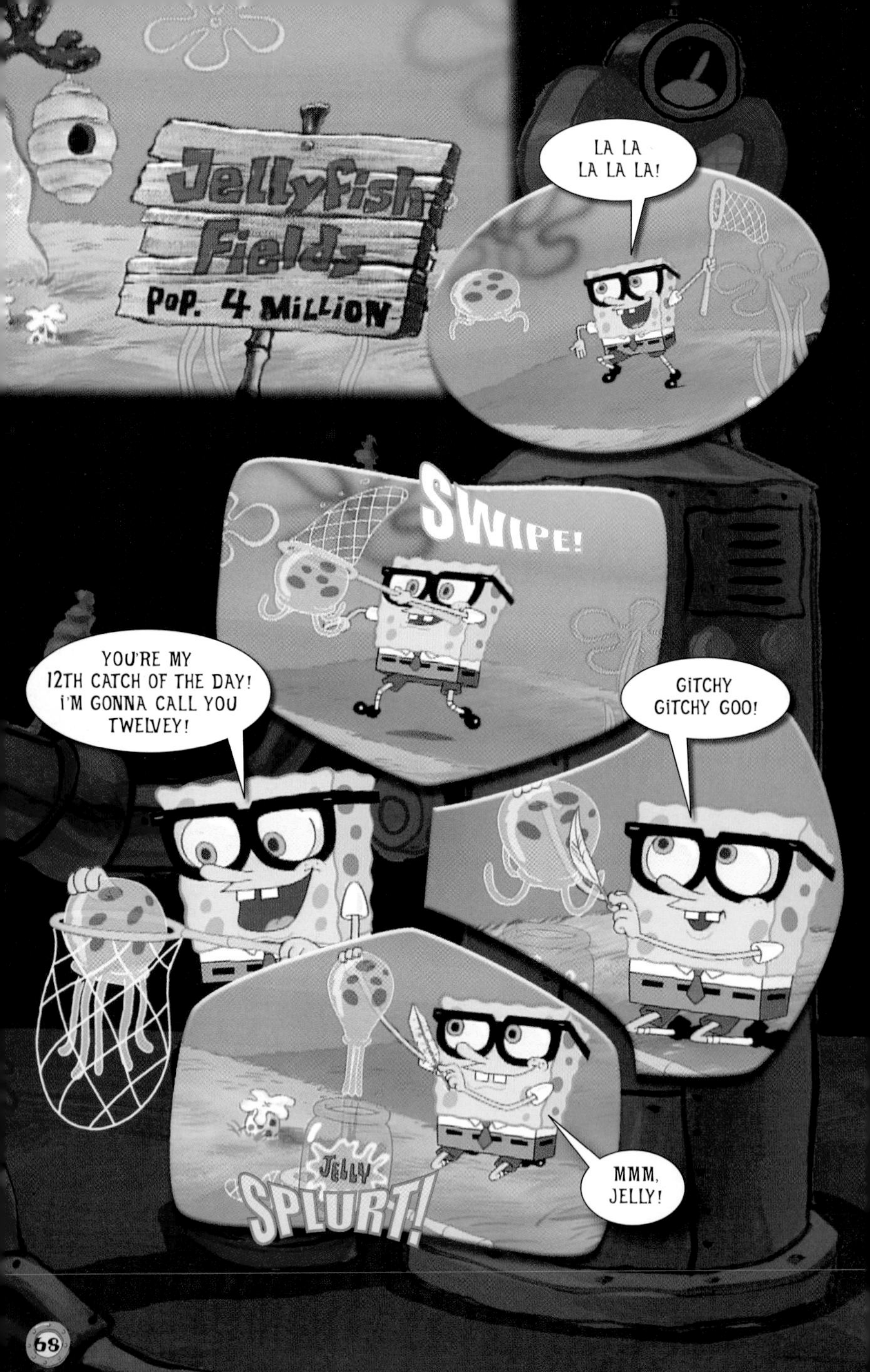
Jellyfish Fields
Pop. 4 MILLION
LA LA LA LA LA!
SWIPE!
YOU'RE MY 12TH CATCH OF THE DAY! I'M GONNA CALL YOU TWELVEY!
GITCHY GITCHY GOO!
JELLY
SPLURT!
MMM, JELLY!

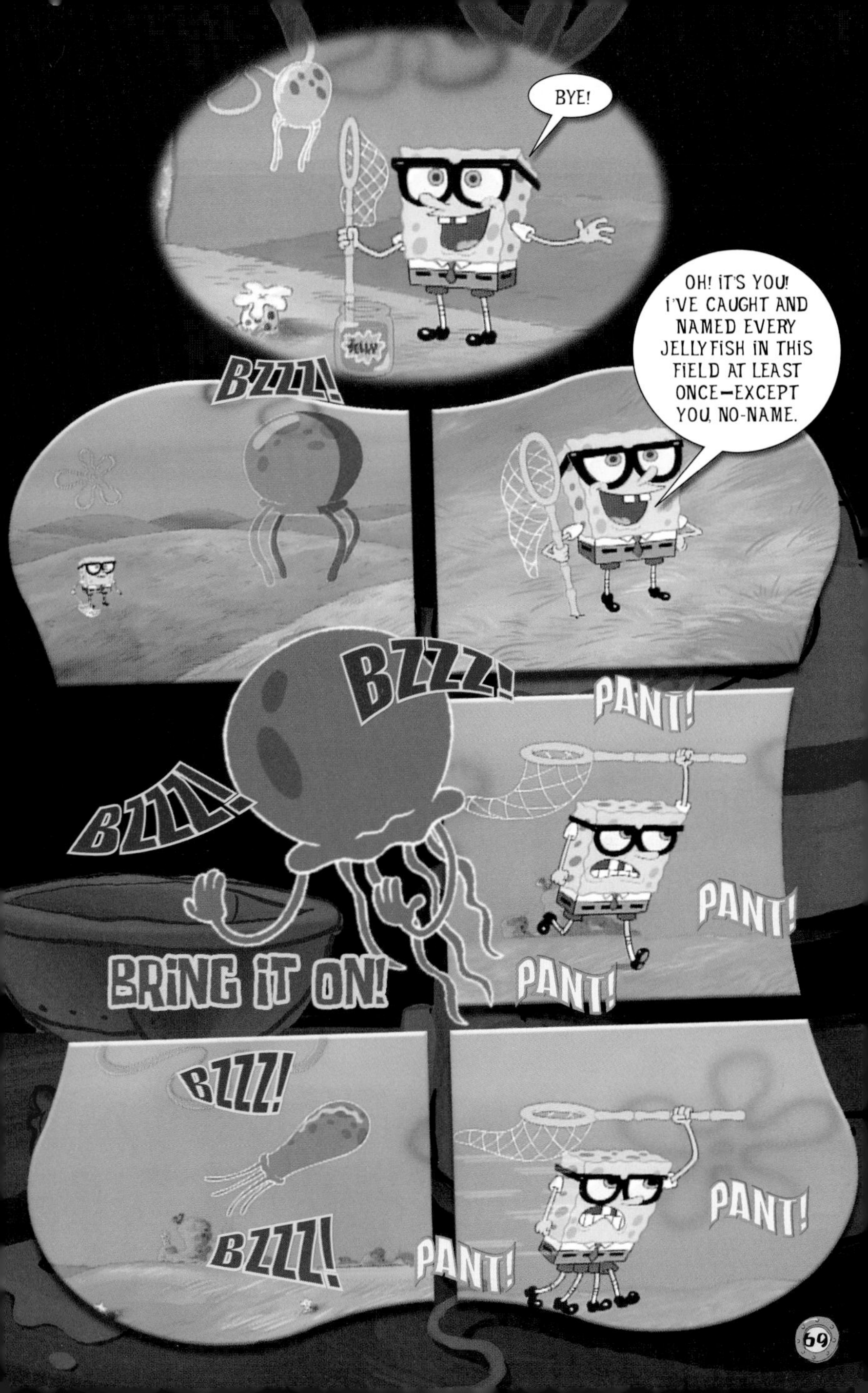

BYE!
BZZZ!
OH! IT'S YOU! I'VE CAUGHT AND NAMED EVERY JELLYFISH IN THIS FIELD AT LEAST ONCE—EXCEPT YOU, NO-NAME.
BZZZ!
BZZZ!
BRING IT ON!
PANT!
PANT!
PANT!
BZZZ!
BZZZ!
PANT!
PANT!

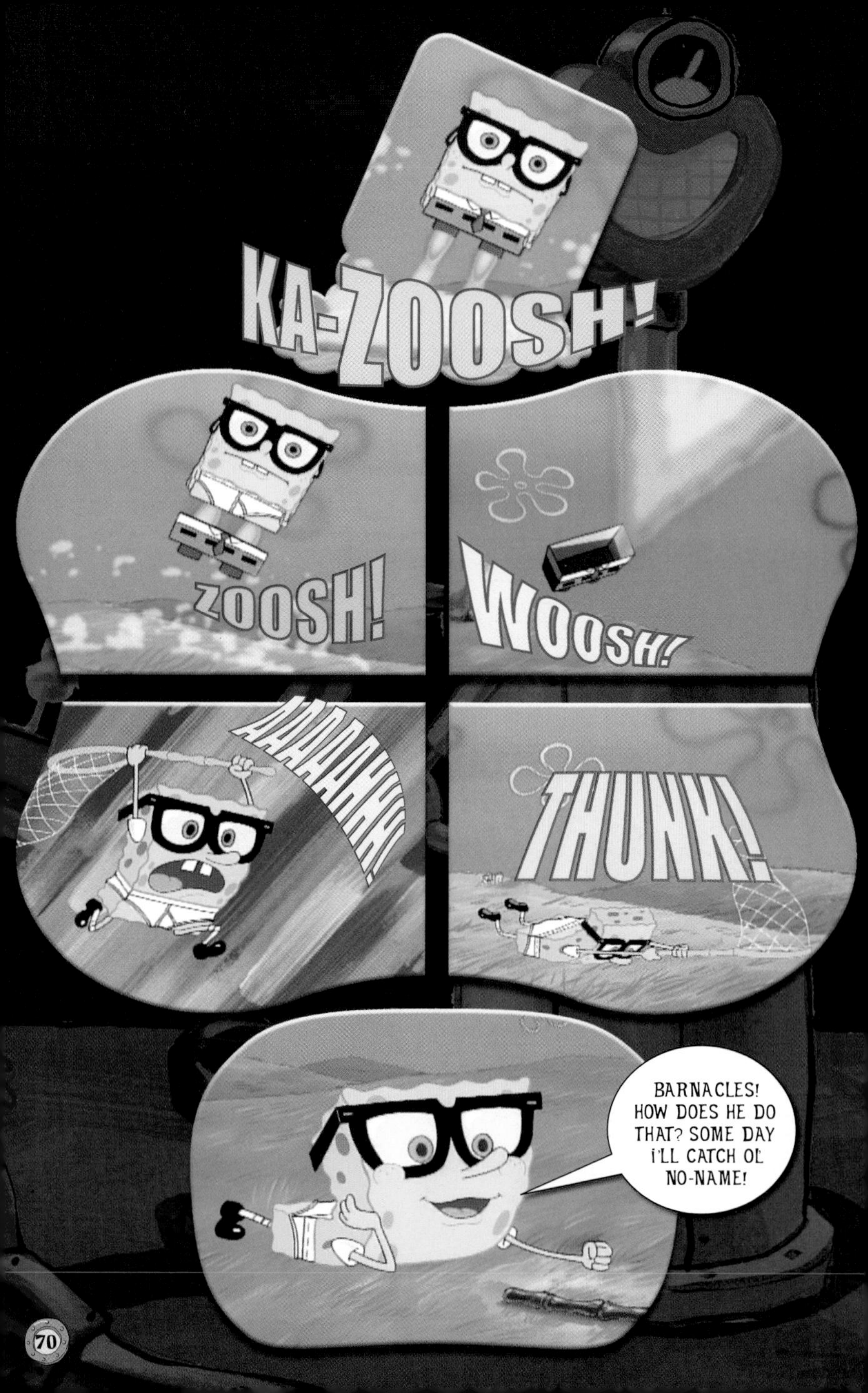
KA-ZOOSH!
ZOOSH!
WOOSH!
THUNK!
BARNACLES! HOW DOES HE DO THAT? SOME DAY I'LL CATCH OL' NO-NAME!

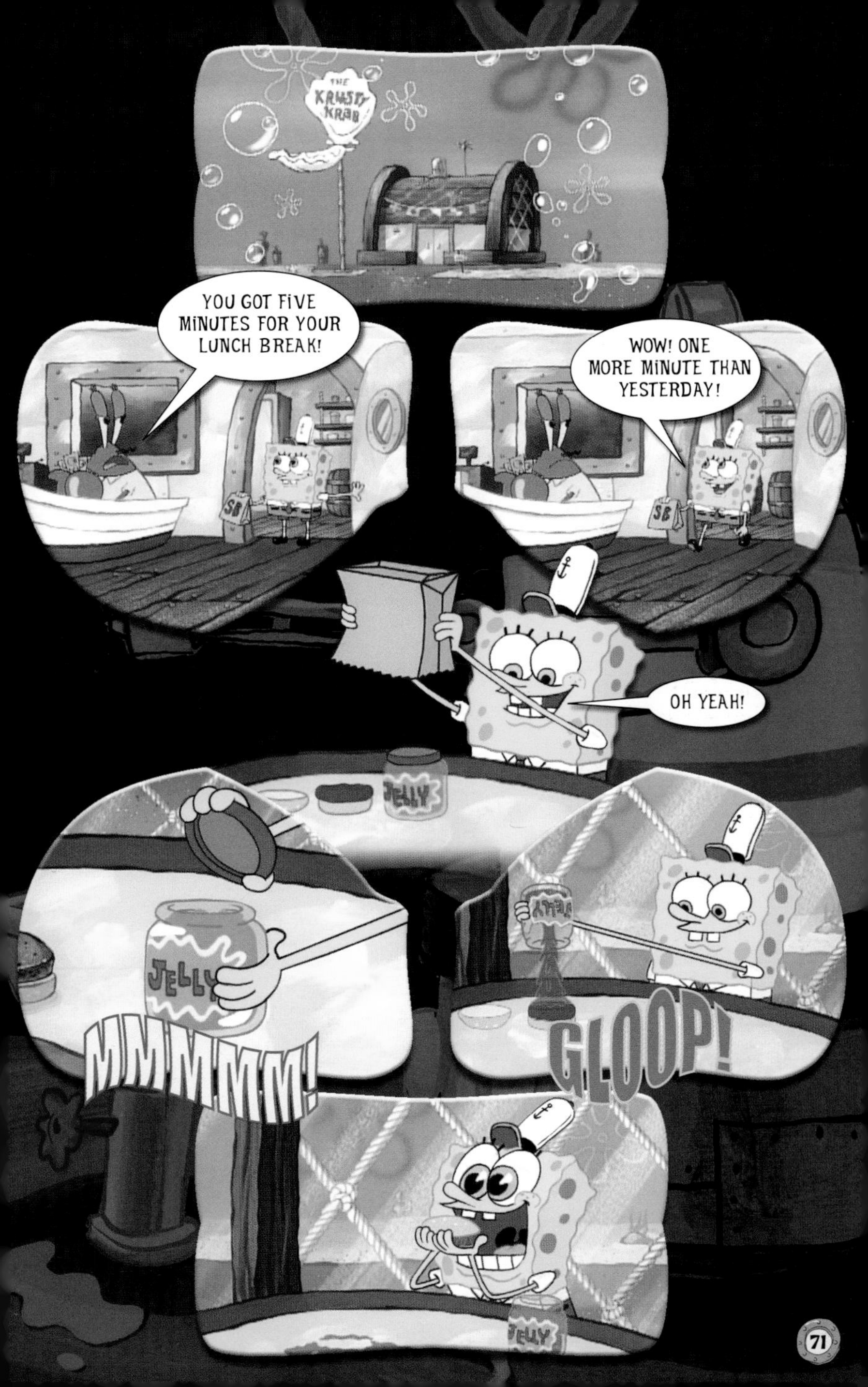
THE KRUSTY KRAB
YOU GOT FIVE MINUTES FOR YOUR LUNCH BREAK!
WOW! ONE MORE MINUTE THAN YESTERDAY!
SB
SB
OH YEAH!
JELLY
JELLY
MMMMMM!
GLOOP!
JELLY

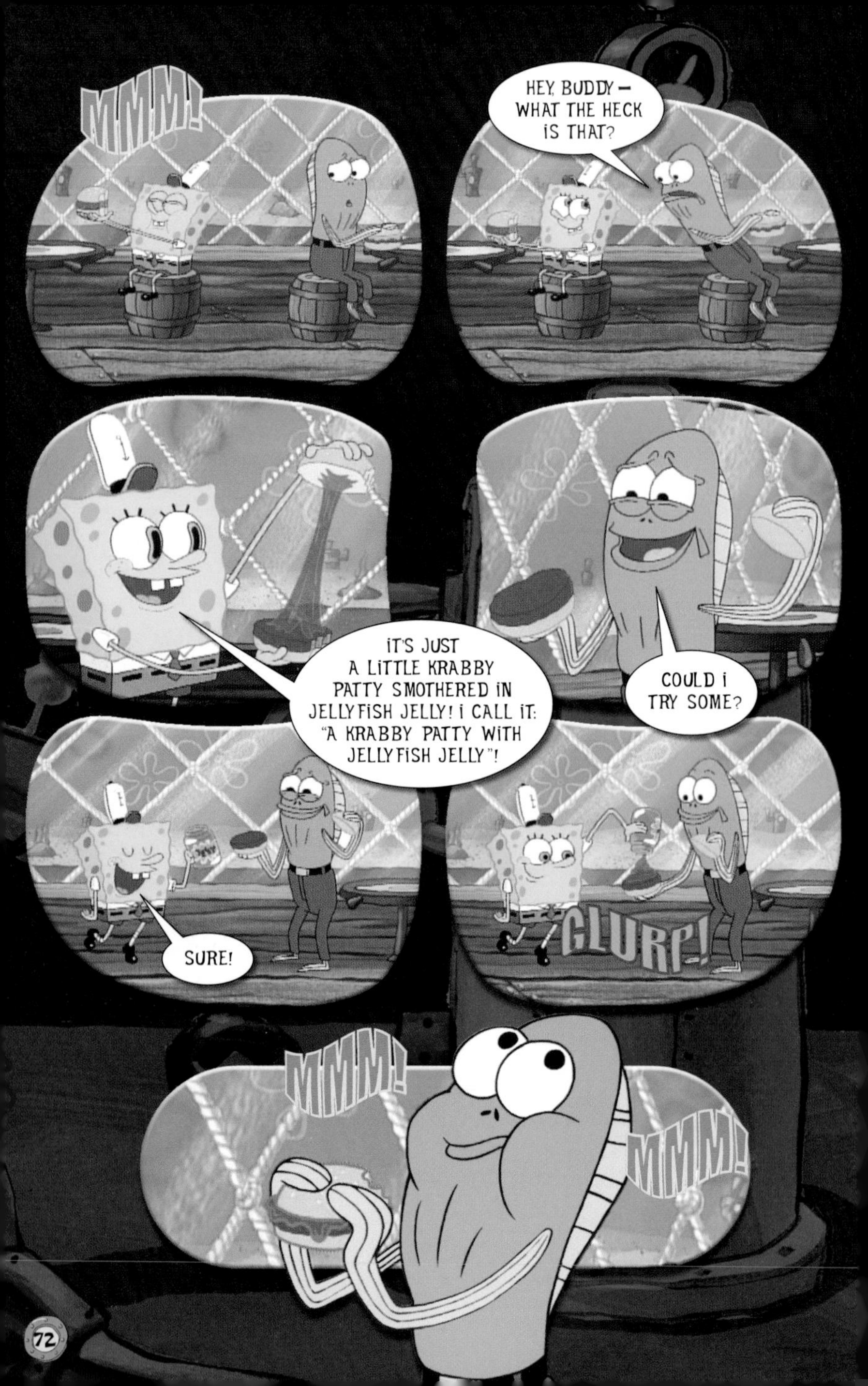
MMM!
HEY, BUDDY — WHAT THE HECK IS THAT?
IT'S JUST A LITTLE KRABBY PATTY SMOTHERED IN JELLYFISH JELLY! I CALL IT: "A KRABBY PATTY WITH JELLYFISH JELLY"!
COULD I TRY SOME?
SURE!
GLURP!
MMM!
MMM!

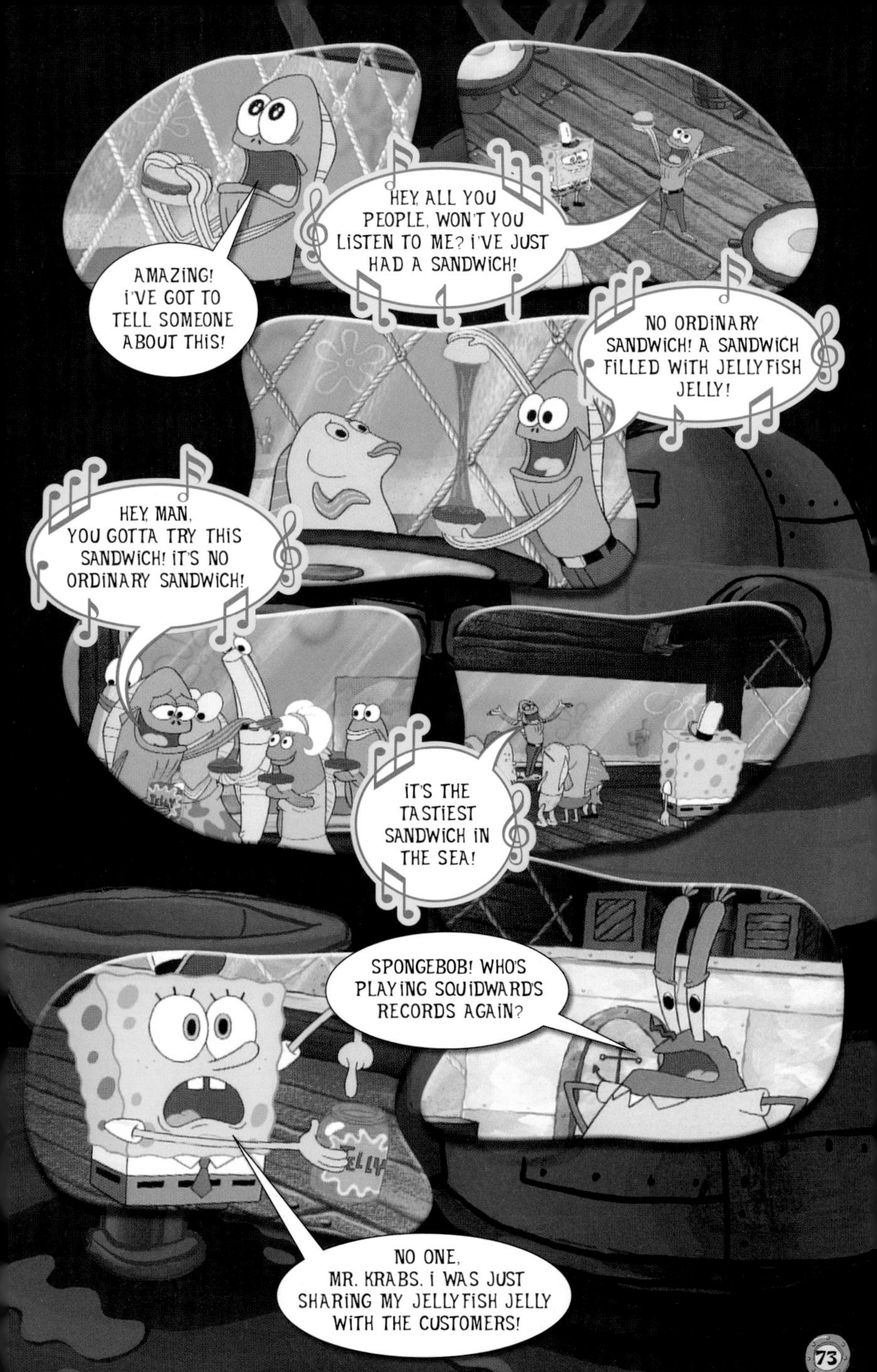
AMAZING! I'VE GOT TO TELL SOMEONE ABOUT THIS!
HEY, ALL YOU PEOPLE, WON'T YOU LISTEN TO ME? I'VE JUST HAD A SANDWICH!
NO ORDINARY SANDWICH! A SANDWICH FILLED WITH JELLYFISH JELLY!
HEY, MAN, YOU GOTTA TRY THIS SANDWICH! IT'S NO ORDINARY SANDWICH!
IT'S THE TASTIEST SANDWICH IN THE SEA!
SPONGEBOB! WHO'S PLAYING SQUIDWARD'S RECORDS AGAIN?
NO ONE, MR. KRABS. I WAS JUST SHARING MY JELLYFISH JELLY WITH THE CUSTOMERS!

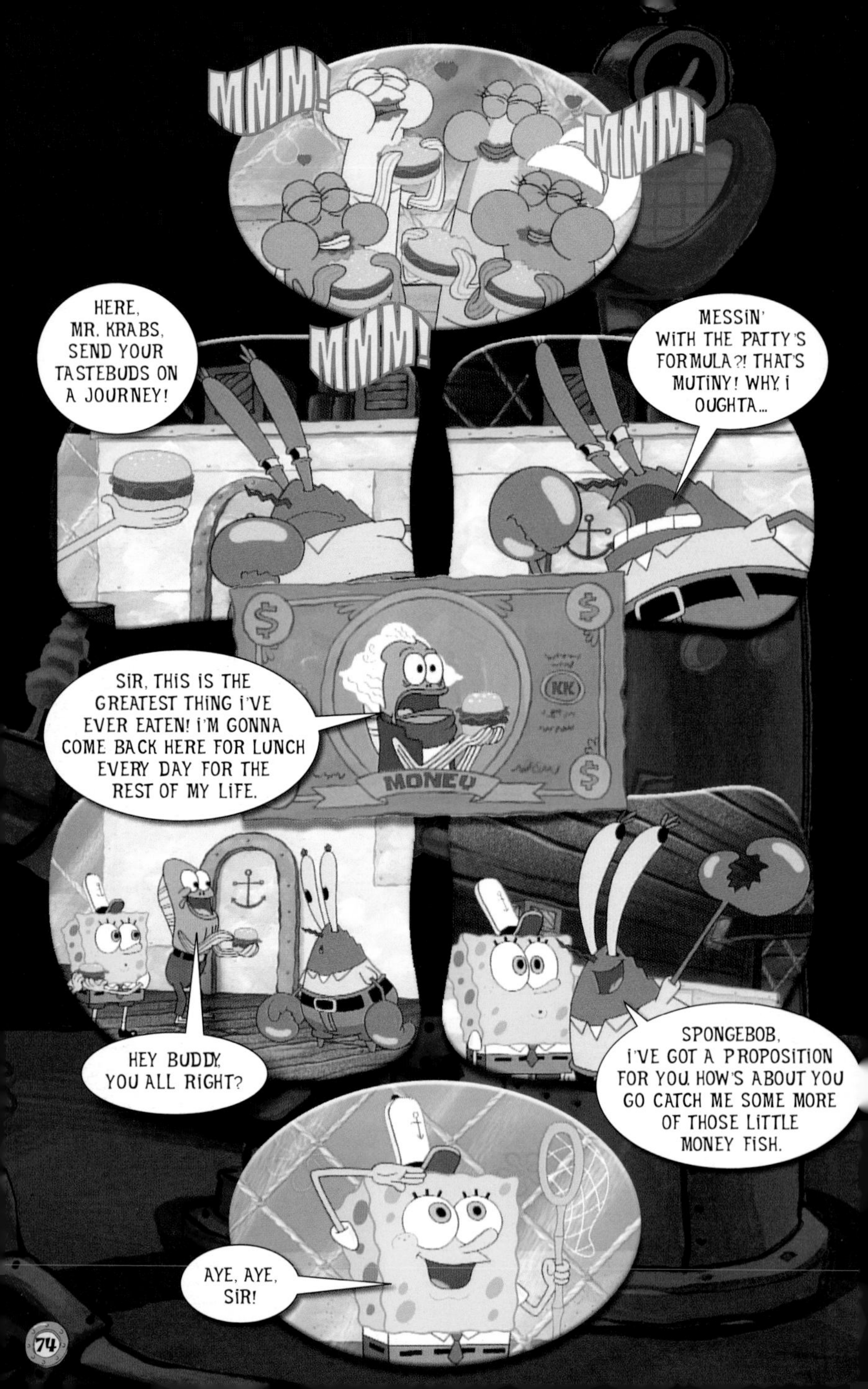
MMM!
MMM!
MMM!
HERE, MR. KRABS, SEND YOUR TASTEBUDS ON A JOURNEY!
MESSIN' WITH THE PATTY'S FORMULA?! THAT'S MUTINY! WHY, I OUGHTA...
MONEY
SIR, THIS IS THE GREATEST THING I'VE EVER EATEN! I'M GONNA COME BACK HERE FOR LUNCH EVERY DAY FOR THE REST OF MY LIFE.
HEY BUDDY, YOU ALL RIGHT?
SPONGEBOB, I'VE GOT A PROPOSITION FOR YOU. HOW'S ABOUT YOU GO CATCH ME SOME MORE OF THOSE LITTLE MONEY FISH.
AYE, AYE, SIR!

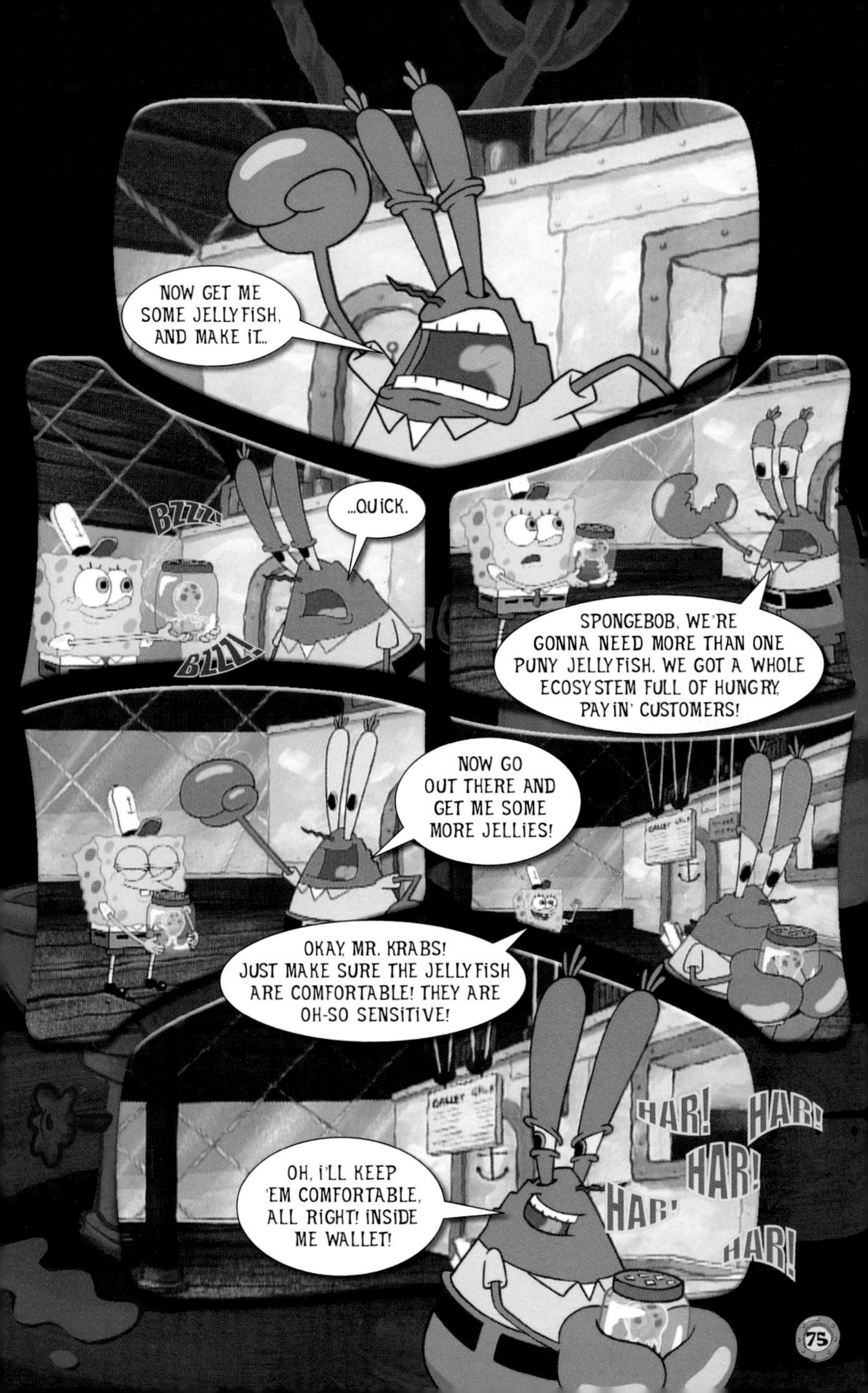
NOW GET ME SOME JELLYFISH, AND MAKE IT...
BZZZ!
...QUICK.
BZZZ!
SPONGEBOB, WE'RE GONNA NEED MORE THAN ONE PUNY JELLYFISH. WE GOT A WHOLE ECOSYSTEM FULL OF HUNGRY, PAYIN' CUSTOMERS!
NOW GO OUT THERE AND GET ME SOME MORE JELLIES!
OKAY, MR. KRABS! JUST MAKE SURE THE JELLYFISH ARE COMFORTABLE! THEY ARE OH-SO SENSITIVE!
OH, I'LL KEEP 'EM COMFORTABLE, ALL RIGHT! INSIDE ME WALLET!
HAR! HAR! HAR! HAR! HAR!

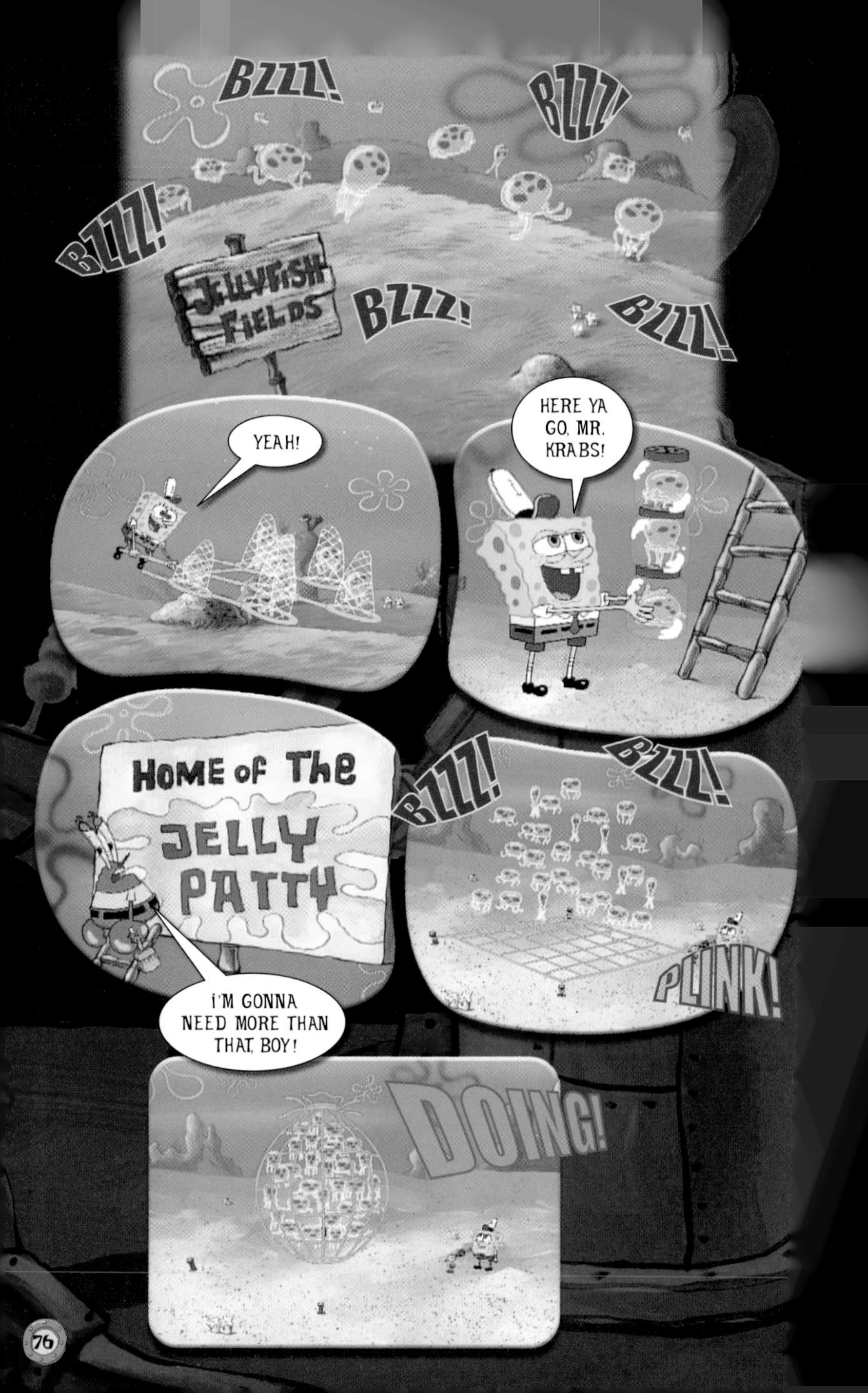
BZZZ!
BZZZ!
BZZZ!
JELLYFISH FIELDS
BZZZ!
BZZZ!
YEAH!
HERE YA GO, MR. KRABS!
HOME of The JELLY PATTY
I'M GONNA NEED MORE THAN THAT, BOY!
BZZZ!
BZZZ!
PLINK!
DOING!

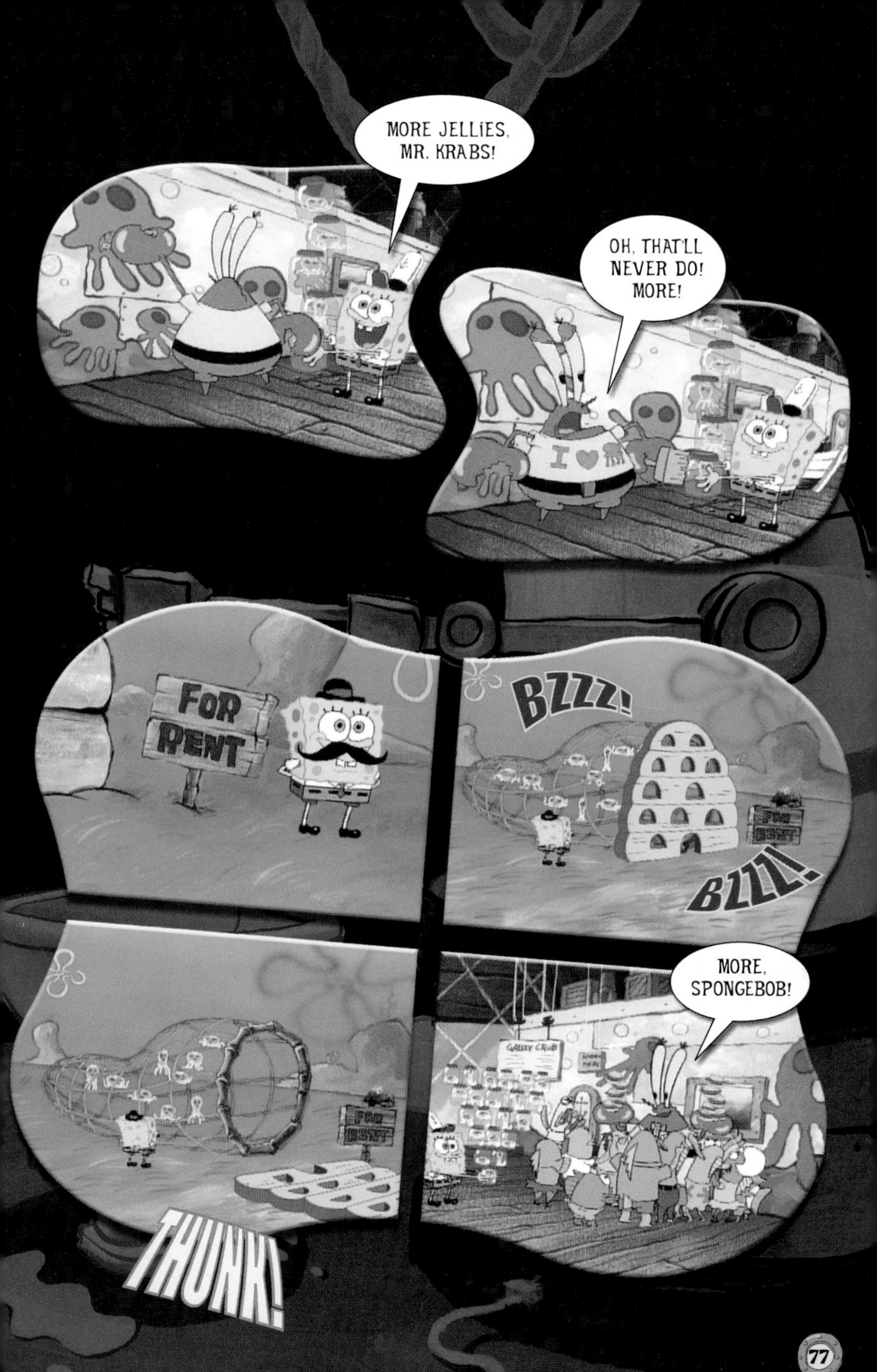
MORE JELLIES, MR. KRABS!
OH, THAT'LL NEVER DO! MORE!
FOR RENT
BZZZ!
BZZZ!
MORE, SPONGEBOB!
THUNK!

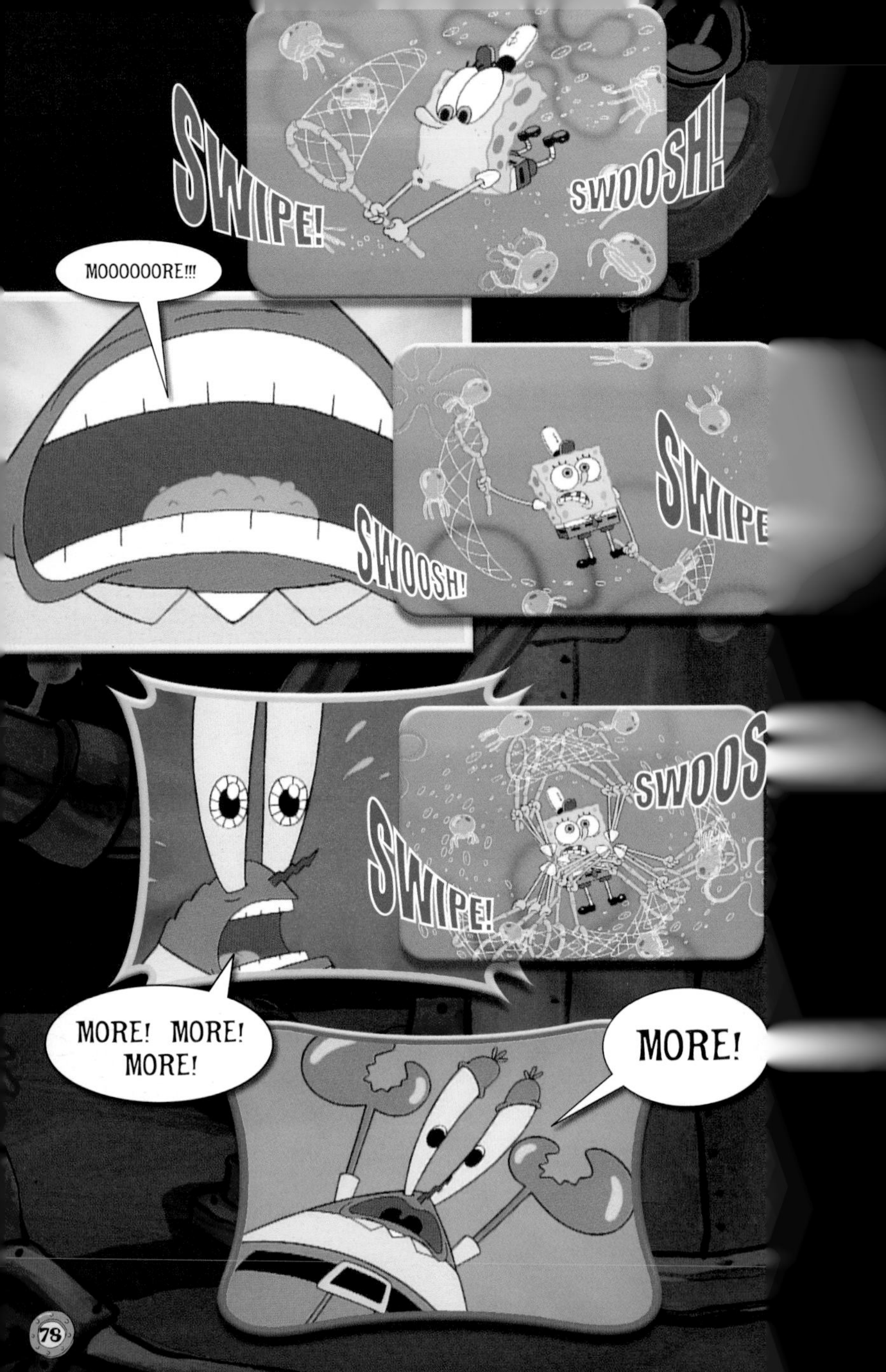
SWIPE!
SWOOSH!
MOOOOOORE!!!
SWOOSH!
SWIPE
SWIPE!
SWOOS
MORE! MORE! MORE!
MORE!

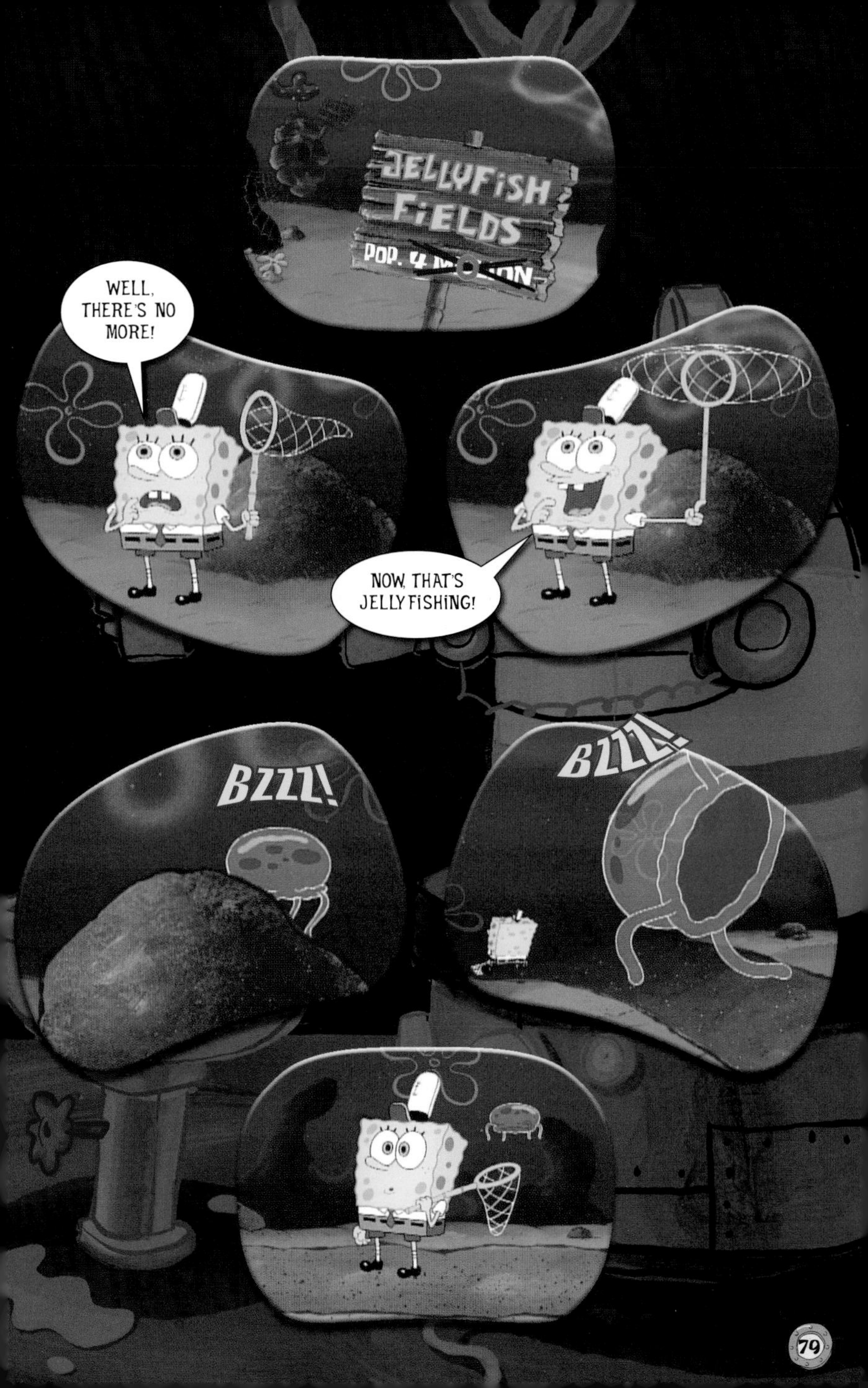
JELLYFISH FIELDS
POP. 4
WELL, THERE'S NO MORE!
NOW, THAT'S JELLYFISHING!
BZZZ!
BZZZ!

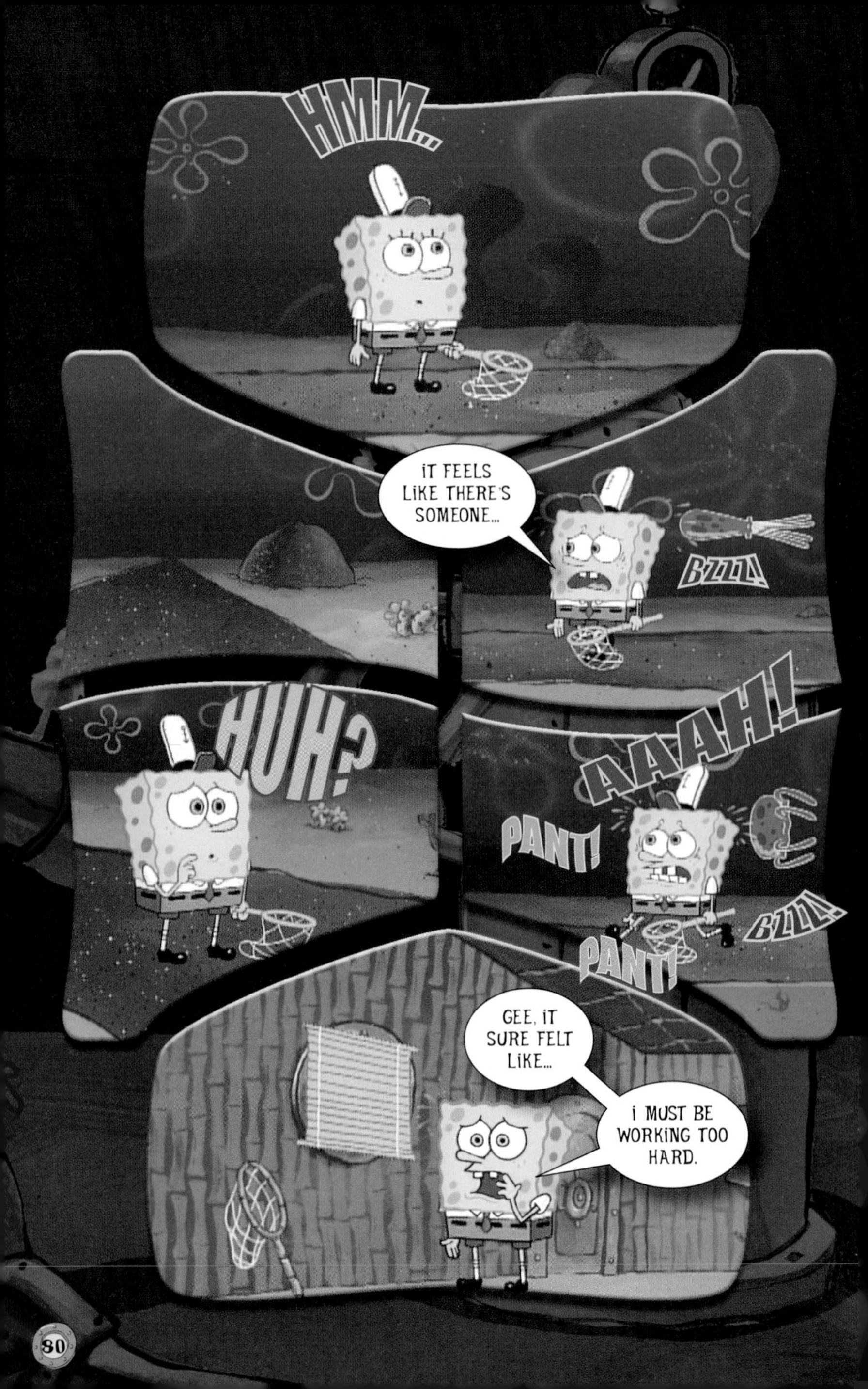
HMM...
IT FEELS LIKE THERE'S SOMEONE...
BZZZ!
HUH?
AAAH!
PANT!
PANT!
BZZZ!
GEE, IT SURE FELT LIKE...
I MUST BE WORKING TOO HARD.

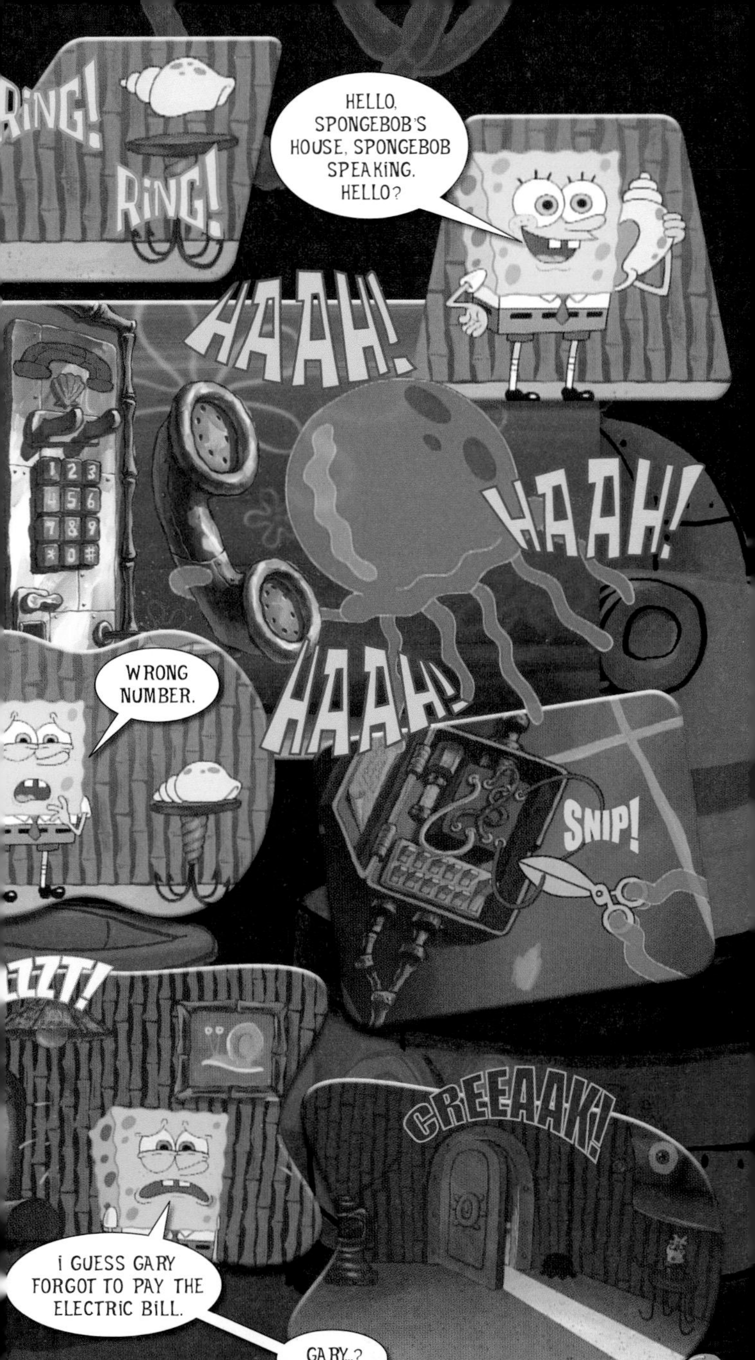
RiNG!
RiNG!
HELLO, SPONGEBOB'S HOUSE, SPONGEBOB SPEAKiNG. HELLO?
HAAAH!
HAAAH!
HAAAH!
WRONG NUMBER.
SNIP!
i GUESS GARY FORGOT TO PAY THE ELECTRiC BiLL.
CREEAAK!
GARY...?

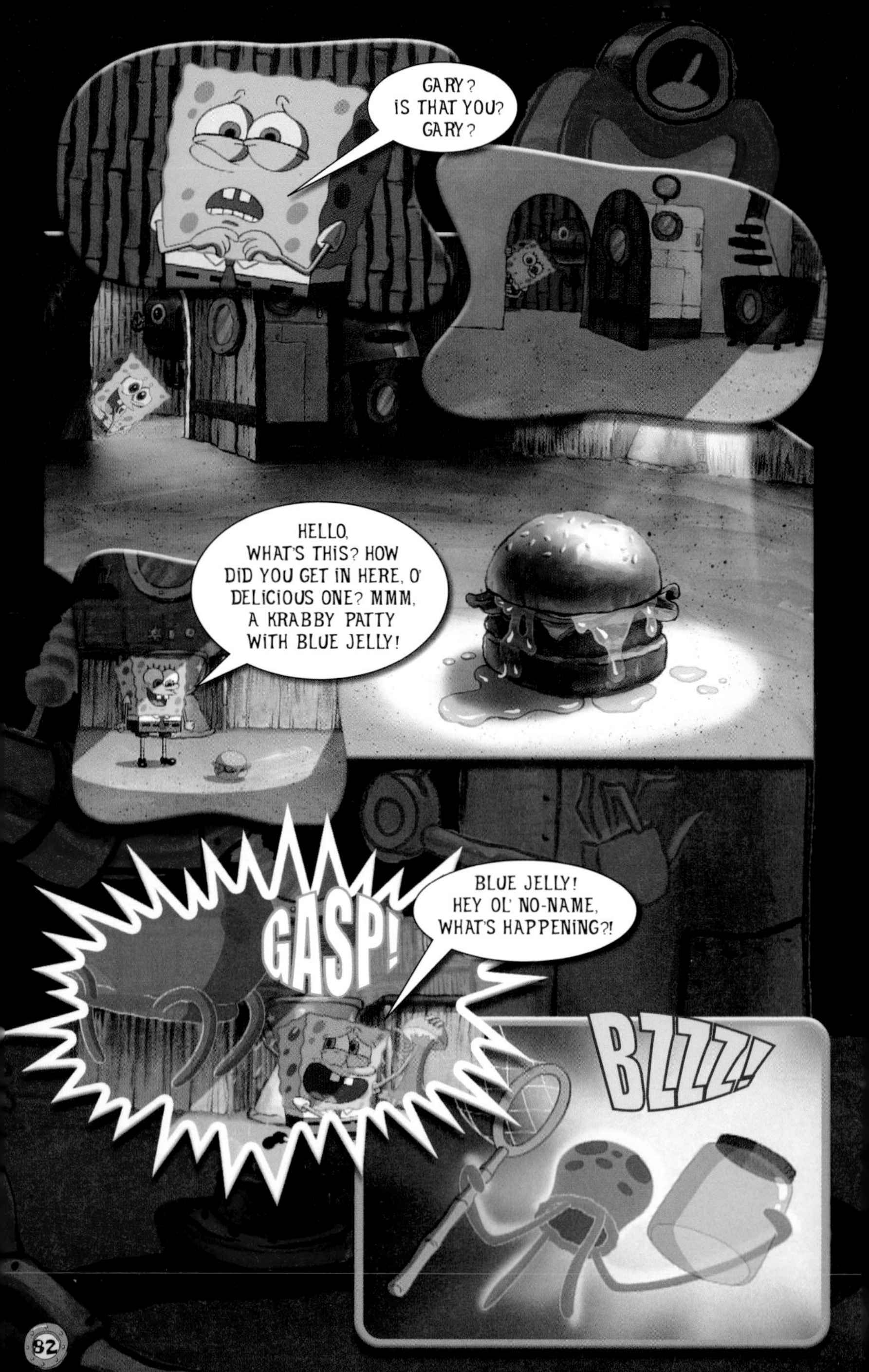
GARY? IS THAT YOU? GARY?
HELLO, WHAT'S THIS? HOW DID YOU GET IN HERE, O' DELICIOUS ONE? MMM, A KRABBY PATTY WITH BLUE JELLY!
GASP!
BLUE JELLY! HEY OL' NO-NAME, WHAT'S HAPPENING?!
BZZZZ!

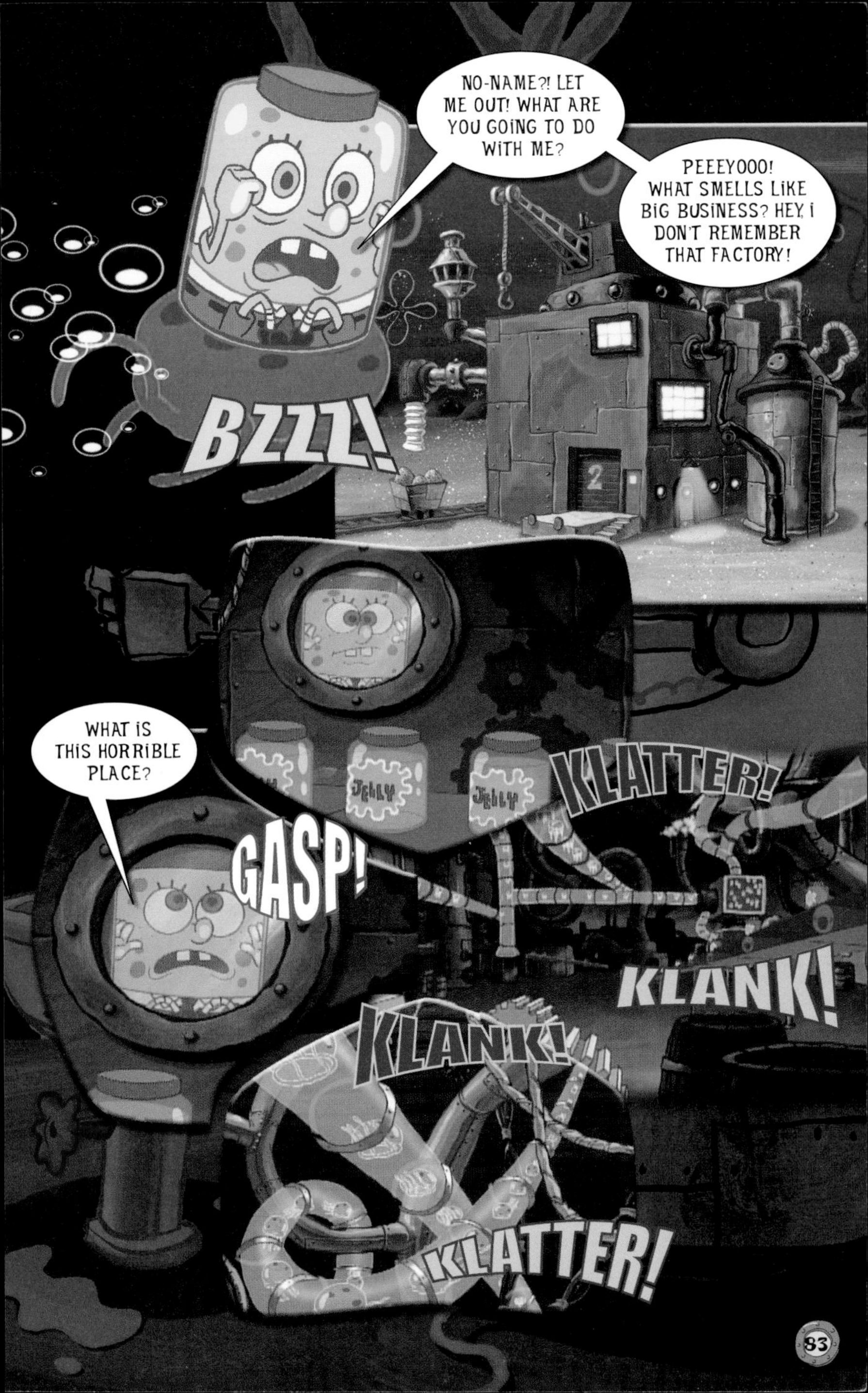
NO-NAME?! LET ME OUT! WHAT ARE YOU GOING TO DO WITH ME?
BZZZ!
PEEEYOOO! WHAT SMELLS LIKE BIG BUSINESS? HEY, I DON'T REMEMBER THAT FACTORY!
2
JELLY
JELLY
WHAT IS THIS HORRIBLE PLACE?
GASP!
KLATTER!
KLANK!
KLANK!
KLATTER!

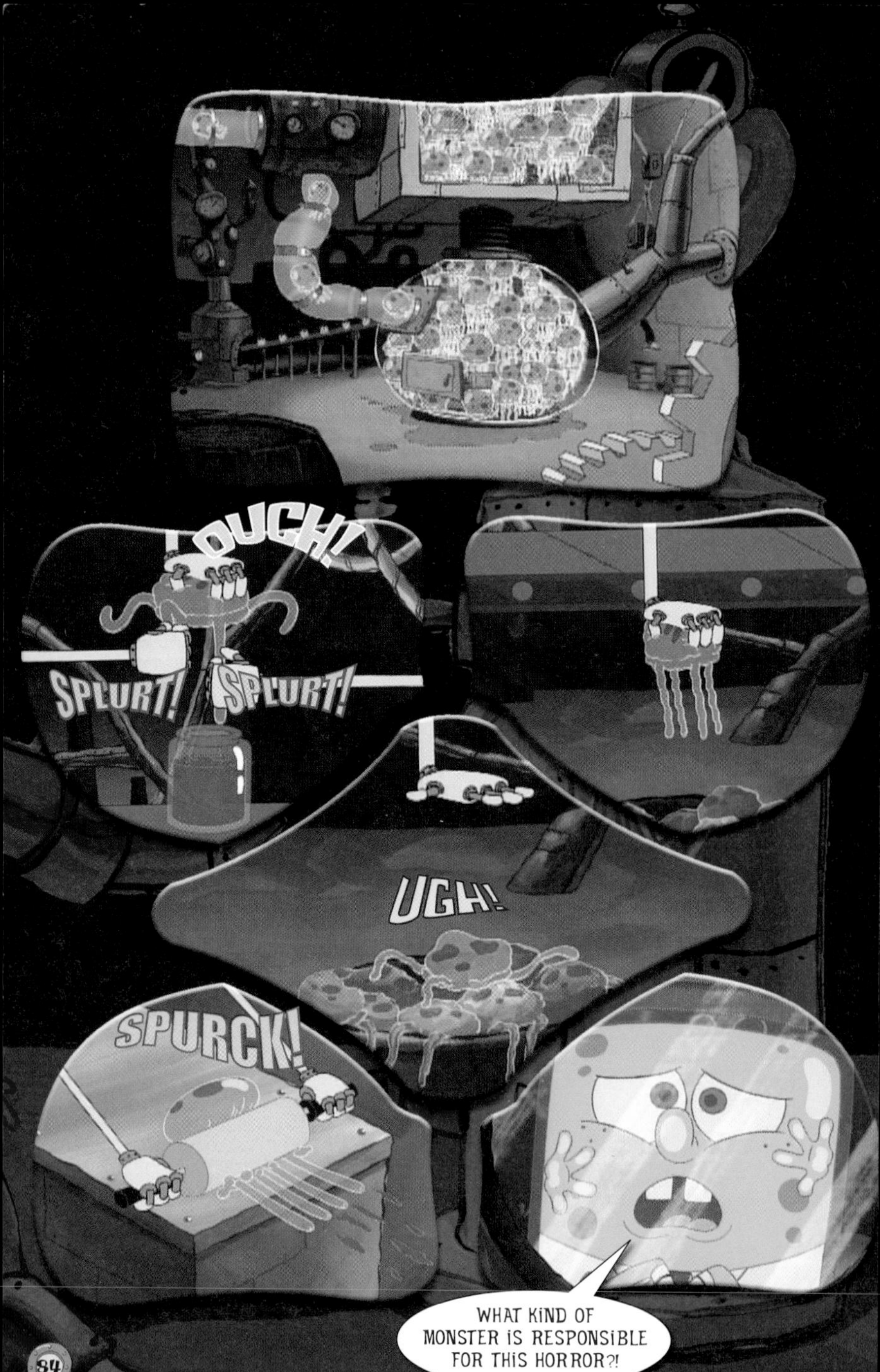
OUCH!
SPLURT!
SPLURT!
UGH!
SPURCK!
WHAT KIND OF MONSTER IS RESPONSIBLE FOR THIS HORROR?!

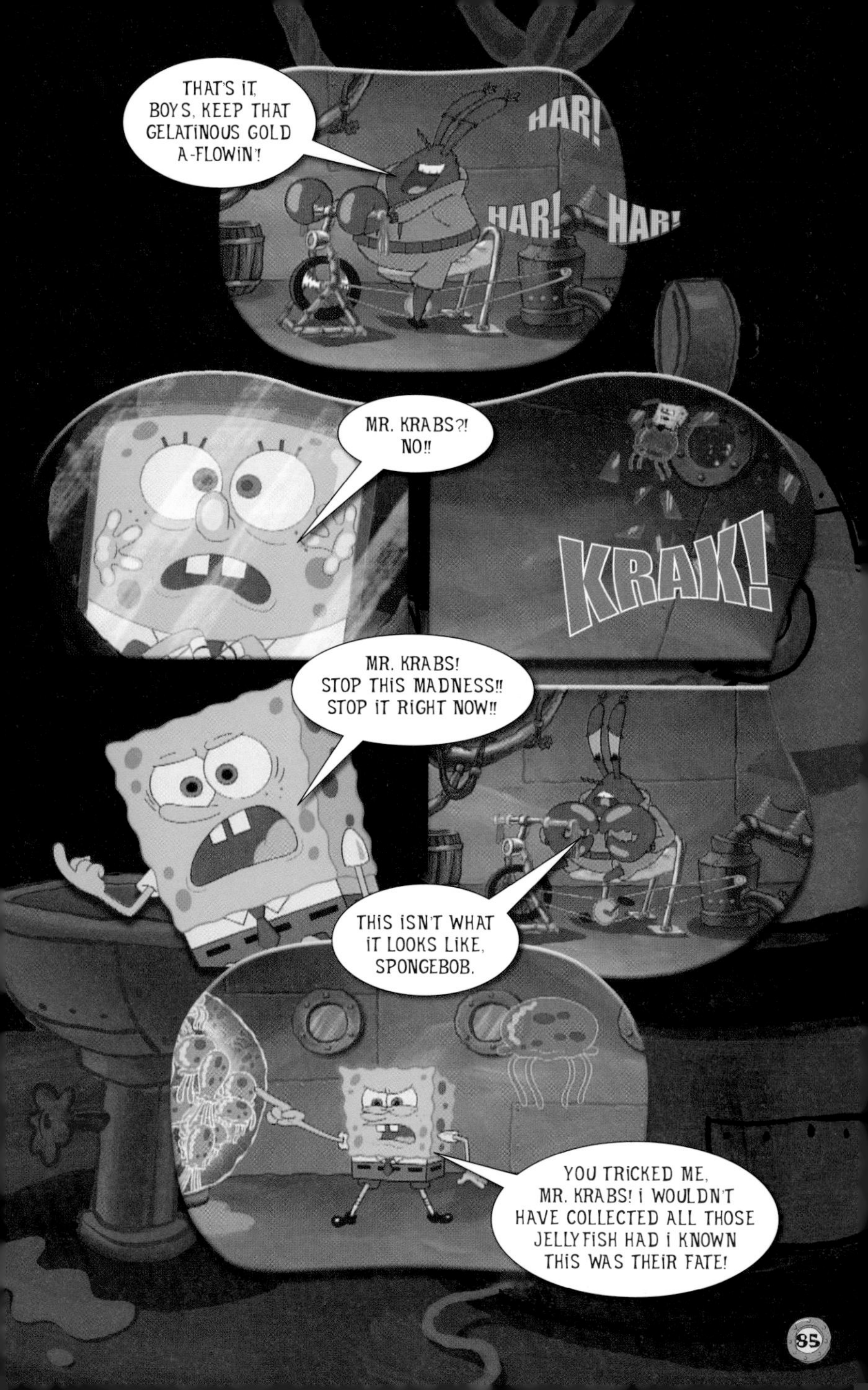

THAT'S IT, BOYS, KEEP THAT GELATINOUS GOLD A-FLOWIN'!
HAR!
HAR!
HAR!
MR. KRABS?! NO!!
KRAK!
MR. KRABS! STOP THIS MADNESS!! STOP IT RIGHT NOW!!
THIS ISN'T WHAT IT LOOKS LIKE, SPONGEBOB.
YOU TRICKED ME, MR. KRABS! I WOULDN'T HAVE COLLECTED ALL THOSE JELLYFISH HAD I KNOWN THIS WAS THEIR FATE!

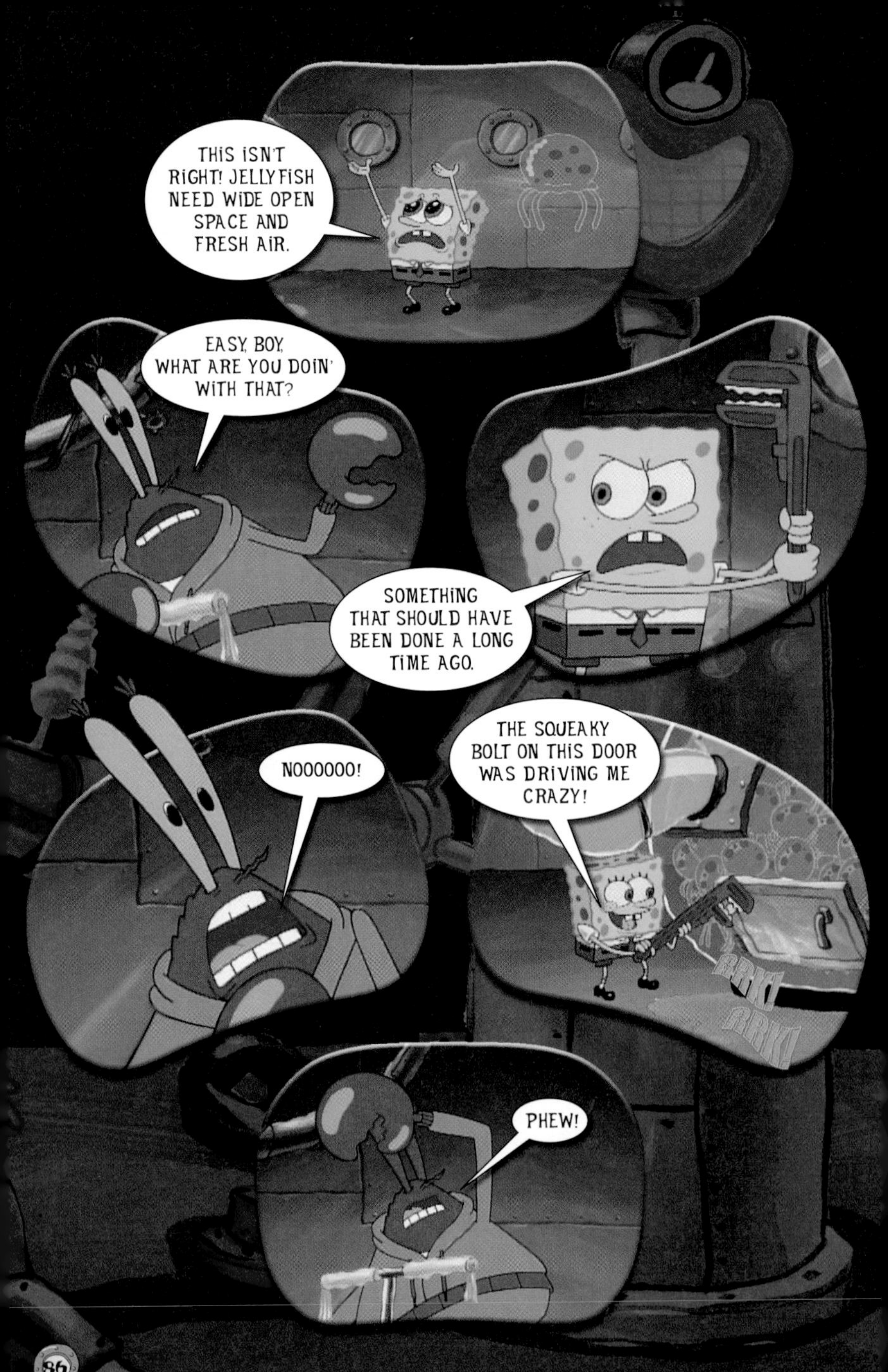
THIS ISN'T RIGHT! JELLYFISH NEED WIDE OPEN SPACE AND FRESH AIR.
EASY, BOY, WHAT ARE YOU DOIN' WITH THAT?
SOMETHING THAT SHOULD HAVE BEEN DONE A LONG TIME AGO.
NOOOOOO!
THE SQUEAKY BOLT ON THIS DOOR WAS DRIVING ME CRAZY!
PHEW!

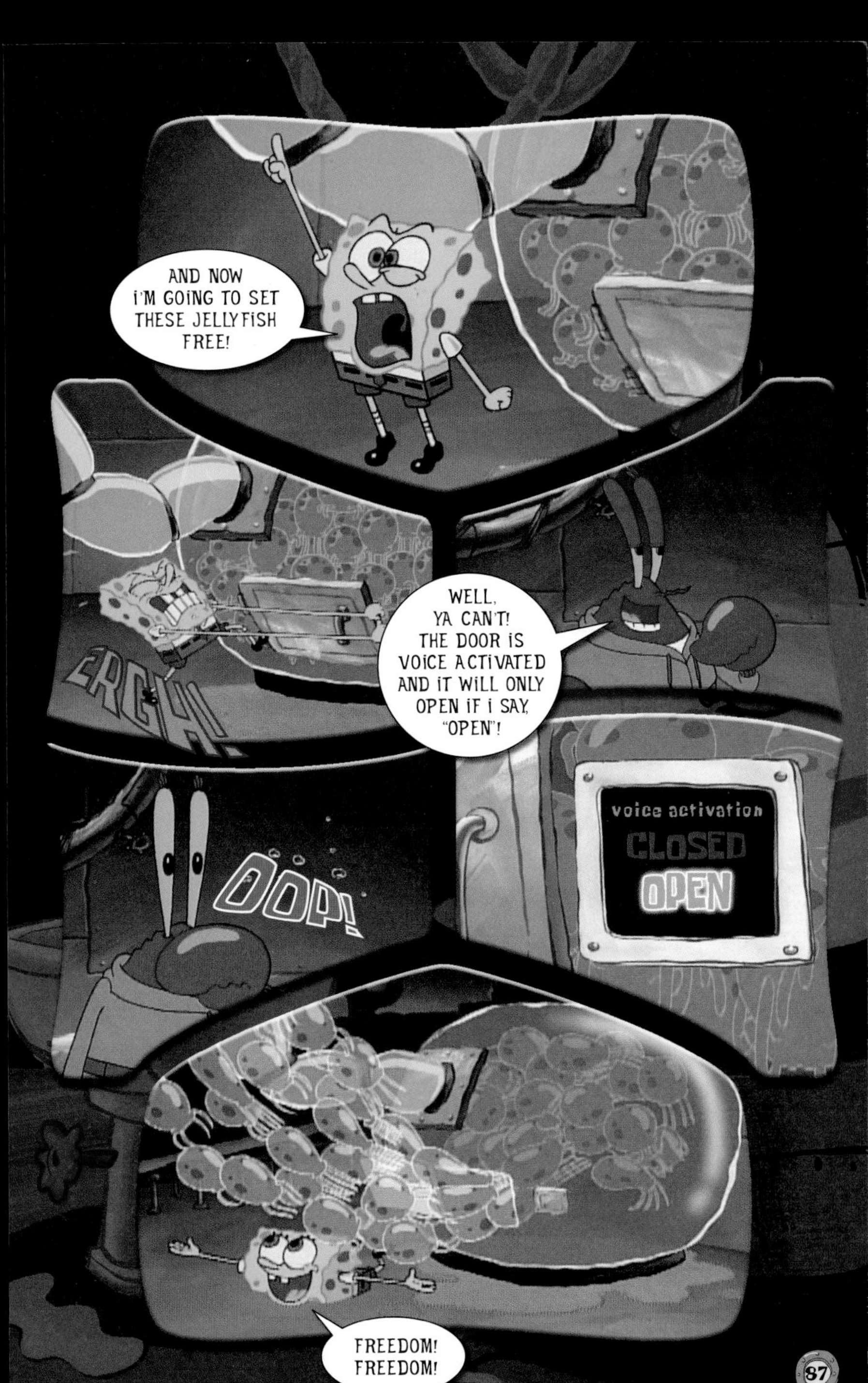
AND NOW
I'M GOING TO SET
THESE JELLYFISH
FREE!
ERGH!
WELL,
YA CAN'T!
THE DOOR IS
VOICE ACTIVATED
AND IT WILL ONLY
OPEN IF I SAY,
"OPEN"!
OOP!
voice activation
CLOSED
OPEN
FREEDOM!
FREEDOM!

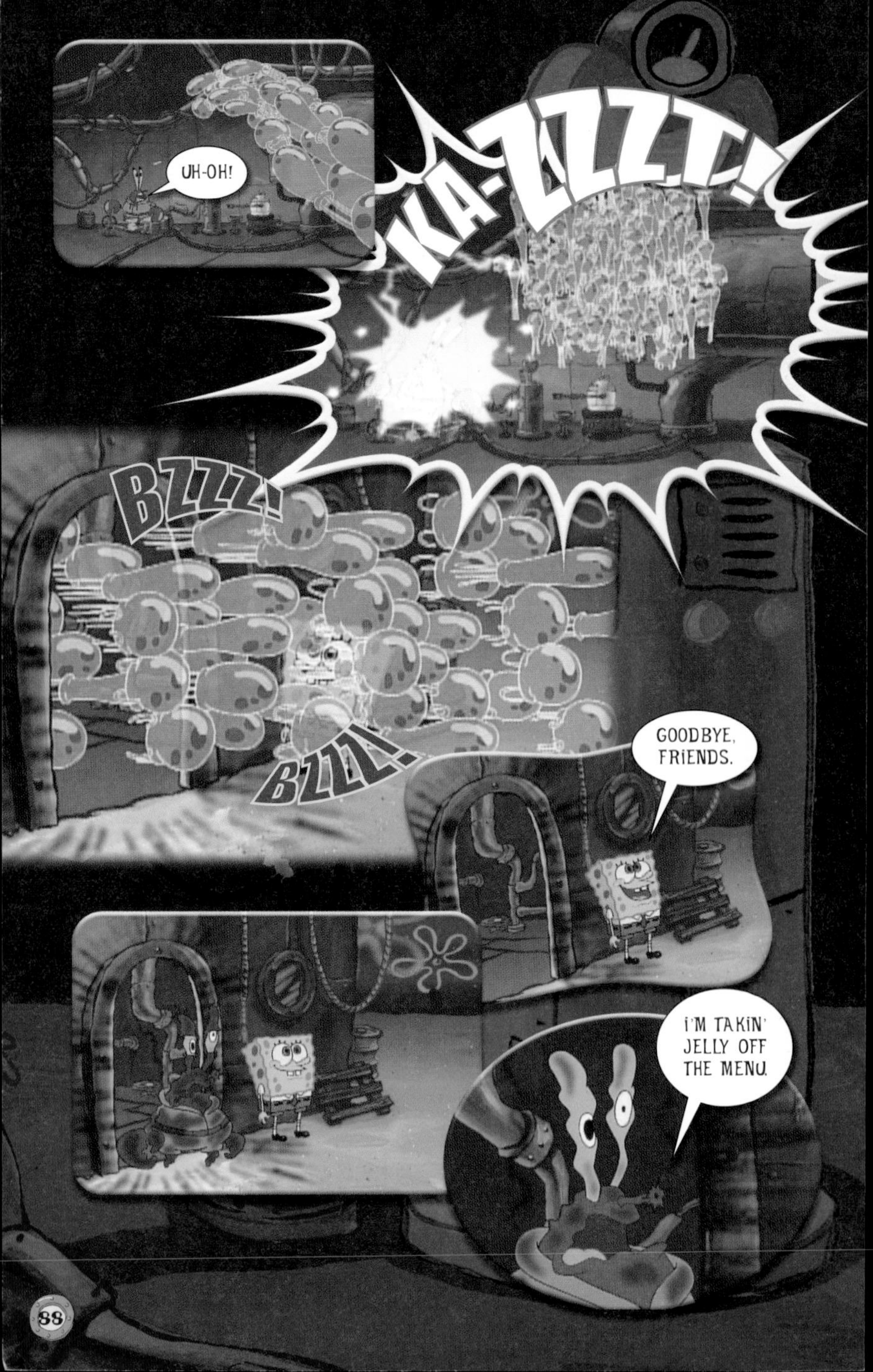
UH-OH!
KA-ZZZZT!
BZZZZ!
BZZZ!
GOODBYE, FRIENDS.
I'M TAKIN' JELLY OFF THE MENU.

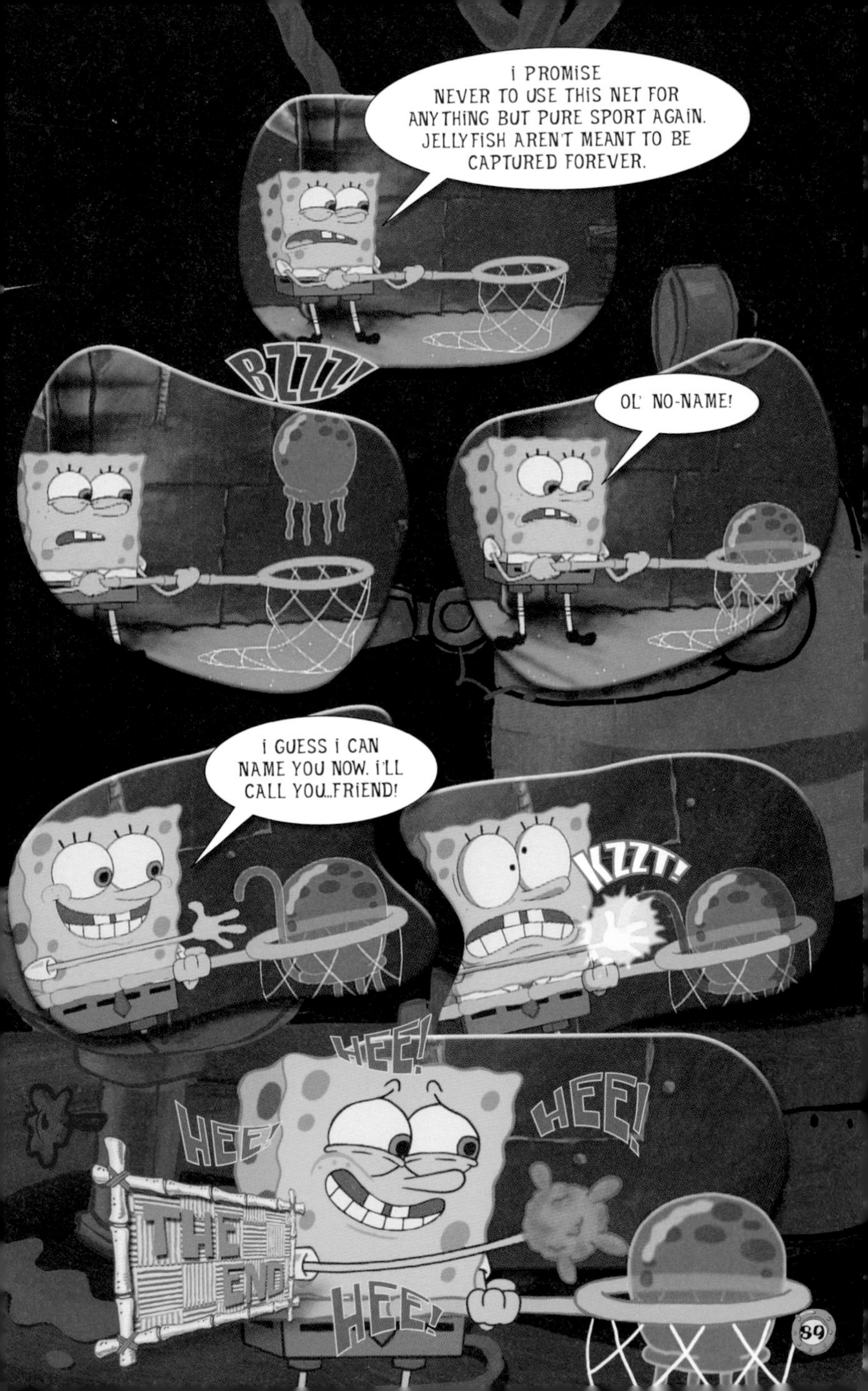
I PROMISE NEVER TO USE THIS NET FOR ANYTHING BUT PURE SPORT AGAIN. JELLYFISH AREN'T MEANT TO BE CAPTURED FOREVER.
BZZZT!
OL' NO-NAME!
I GUESS I CAN NAME YOU NOW. I'LL CALL YOU...FRIEND!
KZZZT!
HEE!
HEE!
HEE!
HEE!
THE END

ALSO AVAILABLE FROM ✪ TOKYOPOP®

MANGA

.HACK//LEGEND OF THE TWILIGHT
ALICHINO
ANGELIC LAYER
BABY BIRTH
BRAIN POWERED
BRIGADOON
B'TX
CANDIDATE FOR GODDESS, THE
CARDCAPTOR SAKURA
CARDCAPTOR SAKURA - MASTER OF THE CLOW
CHRONICLES OF THE CURSED SWORD
CLAMP SCHOOL DETECTIVES
CLOVER
COMIC PARTY
CORRECTOR YUI
COWBOY BEBOP
COWBOY BEBOP: SHOOTING STAR
CRESCENT MOON
CROSS
CULDCEPT
CYBORG 009
D•N•ANGEL
DEARS
DEMON DIARY
DEMON ORORON, THE
DIGIMON
DIGIMON TAMERS
DIGIMON ZERO TWO
DRAGON HUNTER
DRAGON KNIGHTS
DRAGON VOICE
DREAM SAGA
DUKLYON: CLAMP SCHOOL DEFENDERS
ET CETERA
ETERNITY
FAERIES' LANDING
FLCL
FLOWER OF THE DEEP SLEEP
FORBIDDEN DANCE
FRUITS BASKET
G GUNDAM
GATEKEEPERS
GIRL GOT GAME
GUNDAM SEED ASTRAY
GUNDAM SEED ASTRAY R
GUNDAM WING
GUNDAM WING: BATTLEFIELD OF PACIFISTS
GUNDAM WING: ENDLESS WALTZ
GUNDAM WING: THE LAST OUTPOST (G-UNIT)
HANDS OFF!

HARLEM BEAT
HYPER RUNE
I.N.V.U.
INITIAL D
INSTANT TEEN: JUST ADD NUTS
JING: KING OF BANDITS
JING: KING OF BANDITS - TWILIGHT TALES
JULINE
KARE KANO
KILL ME, KISS ME
KINDAICHI CASE FILES, THE
KING OF HELL
KODOCHA: SANA'S STAGE
LAGOON ENGINE
LEGEND OF CHUN HYANG, THE
LILING-PO
LOVE OR MONEY
MAGIC KNIGHT RAYEARTH I
MAGIC KNIGHT RAYEARTH II
MAN OF MANY FACES
MARMALADE BOY
MARS
MARS: HORSE WITH NO NAME
MINK
MIRACLE GIRLS
MODEL
MOURYOU KIDEN: LEGEND OF THE NYMPH
NECK AND NECK
ONE
ONE I LOVE, THE
PEACH FUZZ
PEACH GIRL
PEACH GIRL: CHANGE OF HEART
PHD: PHANTASY DEGREE
PITA-TEN
PLANET BLOOD
PLANET LADDER
PLANETES
PRESIDENT DAD
PRINCESS AI
PSYCHIC ACADEMY
QUEEN'S KNIGHT, THE
RAGNAROK
RAVE MASTER
REALITY CHECK
REBIRTH
REBOUND
RISING STARS OF MANGA™,THE
SAILOR MOON
SAINT TAIL
SAMURAI GIRL™ REAL BOUT HIGH SCHOOL

10.19.04Y

ALSO AVAILABLE FROM  TOKYOPOP®

SOUL TO SEOUL
SEIKAI TRILOGY, THE
SGT. FROG
SHAOLIN SISTERS
SHIRAHIME-SYO: SNOW GODDESS TALES
SHUTTERBOX
SKULL MAN, THE
SUIKODEN III
SUKI
TAROT CAFÉ, THE
THREADS OF TIME
TOKYO BABYLON
TOKYO MEW MEW
VAMPIRE GAME
WARCRAFT
WISH
WORLD OF HARTZ
ZODIAC P.I.

CINE-MANGA®

ALADDIN
CARDCAPTORS
DUEL MASTERS
FAIRLY ODDPARENTS, THE
FAMILY GUY
FINDING NEMO
G.I. JOE SPY TROOPS
GREATEST STARS OF THE NBA
JACKIE CHAN ADVENTURES
JIMMY NEUTRON: BOY GENIUS, THE ADVENTURES OF
KIM POSSIBLE
LILO & STITCH: THE SERIES
LIZZIE MCGUIRE
LIZZIE MCGUIRE MOVIE, THE
MALCOLM IN THE MIDDLE
POWER RANGERS: DINO THUNDER
POWER RANGERS: NINJA STORM
PRINCESS DIARIES 2, THE
RAVE MASTER
SHREK 2
SIMPLE LIFE, THE
SPONGEBOB SQUAREPANTS
SPY KIDS 2
SPY KIDS 3-D: GAME OVER
TEENAGE MUTANT NINJA TURTLES
THAT'S SO RAVEN
TOTALLY SPIES
TRANSFORMERS: ARMADA
TRANSFORMERS: ENERGON

NOVELS

CLAMP SCHOOL PARANORMAL INVESTIGATORS
SAILOR MOON
SLAYERS

ART BOOKS

ART OF CARDCAPTOR SAKURA
ART OF MAGIC KNIGHT RAYEARTH, THE
PEACH: MIWA UEDA ILLUSTRATIONS

ANIME GUIDES

COWBOY BEBOP
GUNDAM TECHNICAL MANUALS
SAILOR MOON SCOUT GUIDES

TOKYOPOP KIDS

STRAY SHEEP

You want it? We got it!
A full range of TOKYOPOP
products are available **now** at:
www.TOKYOPOP.com/shop

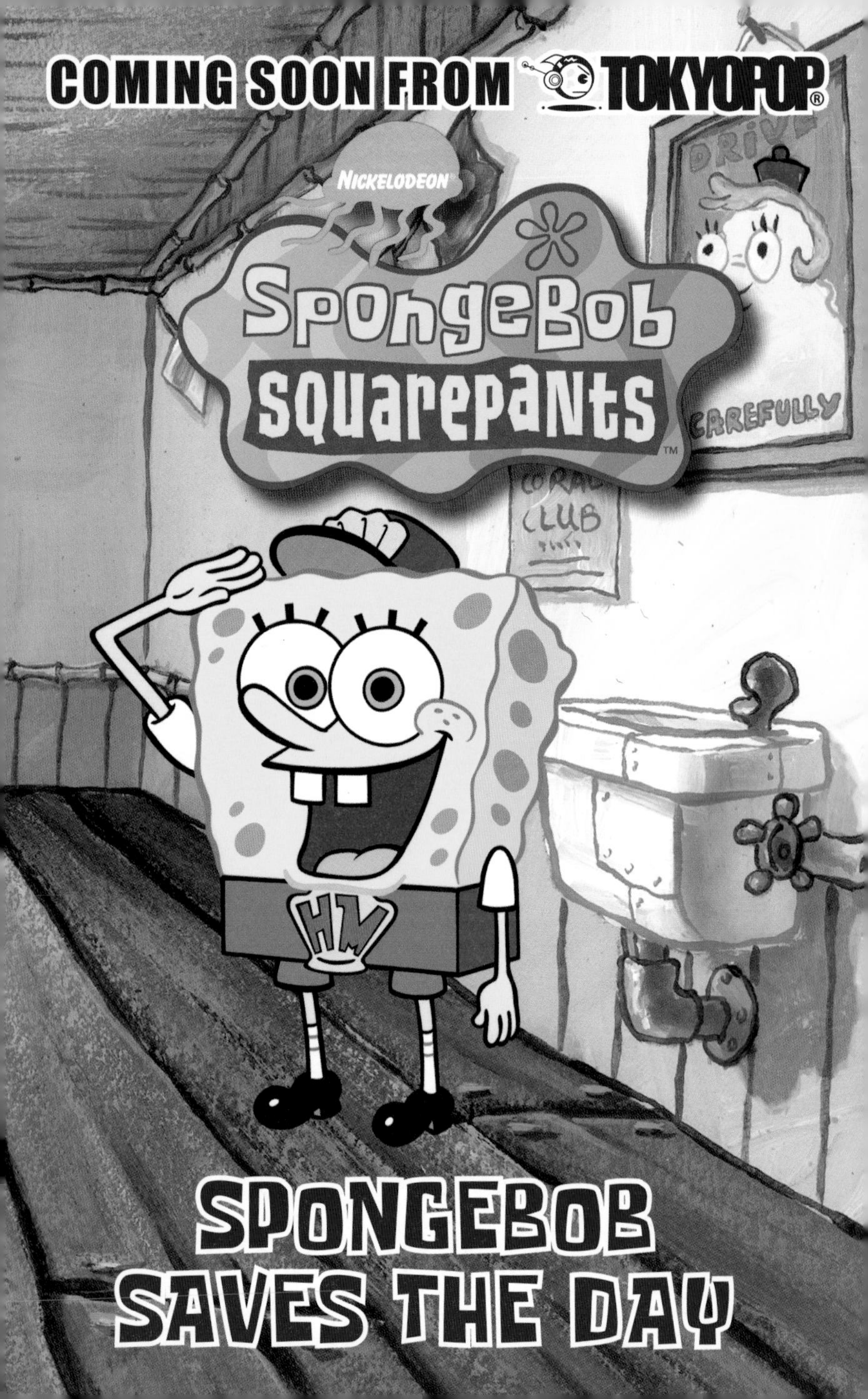
COMING SOON FROM TOKYOPOP®
NICKELODEON
SpongeBob SquarePants™
CAREFULLY
SPONGEBOB SAVES THE DAY

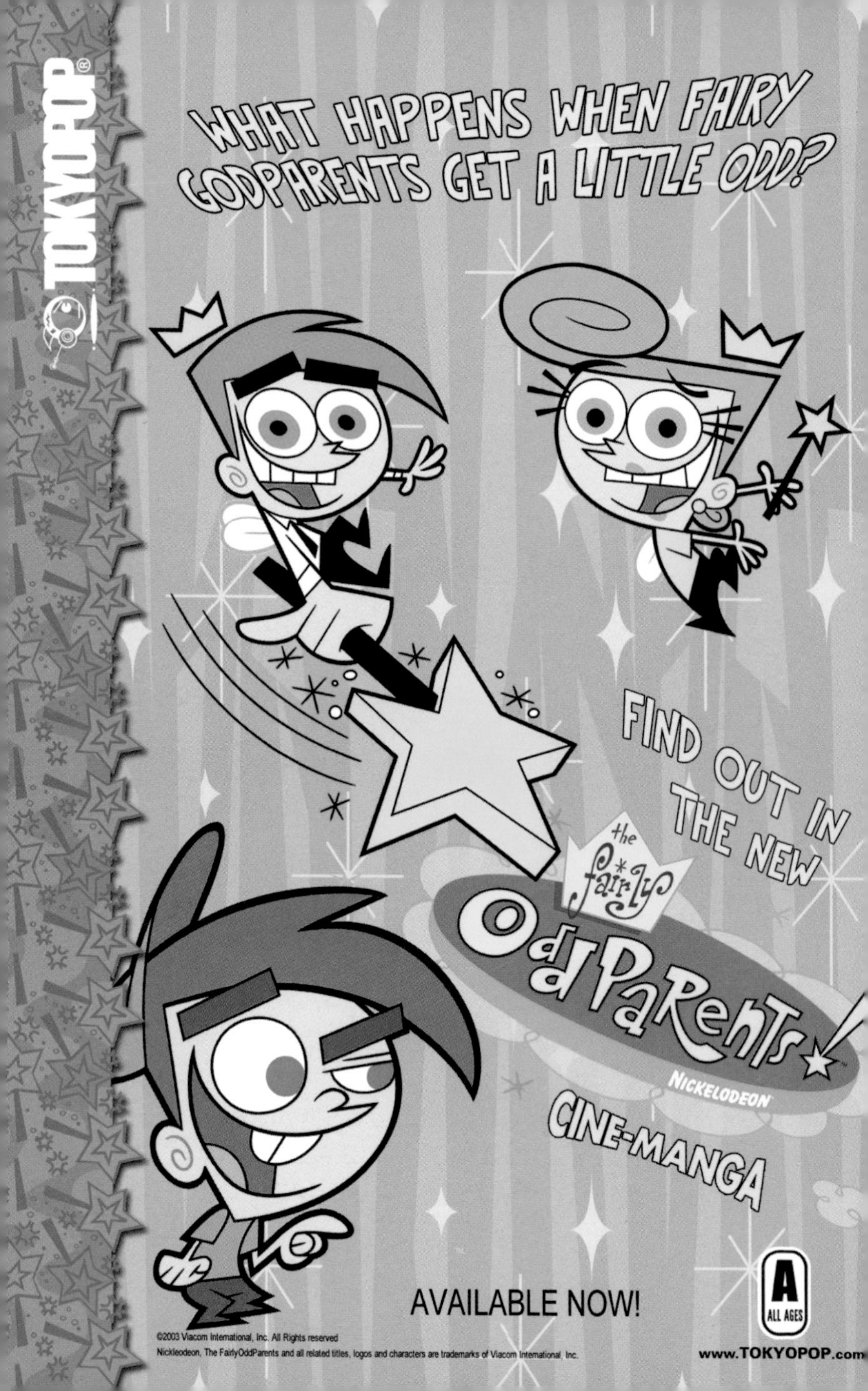
TOKYOPOP
WHAT HAPPENS WHEN FAIRY GODPARENTS GET A LITTLE ODD?
FIND OUT IN THE NEW
the fairly OddParents!
NICKELODEON
CINE-MANGA
AVAILABLE NOW!
A
ALL AGES
©2003 Viacom International, Inc. All Rights reserved
Nickleodeon, The FairlyOddParents and all related titles, logos and characters are trademarks of Viacom International, Inc.
www.TOKYOPOP.com

NICKELODEON®

Introducing a brand new way to use your Game Boy® Advance!

Now you can watch your favorite shows on the #1 portable gaming system--it's full color video that goes with you, anywhere you go!

You can look for all your favorite Nicktoons on Game Boy Advance Video!!

Available now at a store near you.

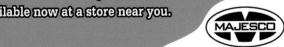

www.gba-video.com